INNER CITY SISSY

David B. Green Jr

INNER CITY SISSY

A Black Queer Literacy Story

**The Queer and LGBT+
Studies Collection**

Collection Editor

Patrick Thomsen

LP
P
p

First published in 2025 by Lived Places Publishing

The author and editor have made every effort to ensure the accuracy of the information contained in this publication but assume no responsibility for any errors, inaccuracies, inconsistencies, or omissions. Likewise, every effort has been made to contact copyright holders. If any copyright material has been reproduced unwittingly and without permission, the publisher will gladly receive information enabling them to rectify any error or omission in subsequent editions.

Copyright © 2025 Lived Places Publishing

British Library Cataloguing in Publication Data
A CIP record for this book is available from the British Library.

ISBN: 9781916704282 (pbk)
ISBN: 9781916704305 (ePDF)
ISBN: 9781916704299 (ePUB)

Cover design by Fiachra McCarthy
Book design by Rachel Trolove of Twin Trail Design
Typeset by Newgen Publishing, UK

Lived Places Publishing
P.O. Box 1845
47 Echo Avenue
Miller Place, NY 11764

www.livedplacespublishing.com

For my mother,
Who left and returned,
Left again and returned, for good

For my sisters,
Who became sister-mothers,
Never leaving, always there

To my brother,
Whose absence has a profound presence
In my heart, always

To those who gave me a home
In the absence of mother
Thank you

I have come to believe over and over again that what is most important to me must be spoken, made verbal and shared, even at the risk of having it bruised or misunderstood.

—Audre Lorde

Abstract

Inner City Sissy is my story: a story about learning to live with compassion, forgiveness, rage, and fierceness! I draw from my lived experiences as a Black gay man who not only came of age in a southern inner-city in America and defied odds of academic achievement by becoming a college professor, but also endured degrees of family and educational trauma that began the day my mother left for the store and returned years later. In my mother's absence, I relied on my sisters, extended family, school, music, and literature as resources that helped me to process the world's cruelty. By writing my story, I hope to offer the value of critical dialogue and reflection as keys to living a life of survival, healing, and flourishing and yes: love.

Keywords

Literacy, motherhood, Black LGBTQ literature, music, flute, inner-city, Blackness, gay, school, teacher

A note on language

There is strong language in the form of "curse" words.

There is also discussion of domestic violence, bullying, and sexual violence.

They can become overwhelming or too much to process.

During these times, I encourage readers to take a break from reading these passages and write down exactly how this passage triggered previous experiences in their lives.

Sissy is often used as a harmful word when referring to gay boys. I reclaim this term for the power it gave me.

Contents

Learning objectives

- Reflect on the power and purpose of your story.
- Develop forgiveness as a life practice.
- Develop critical dialogue on race, gender, and sexuality bias and prevention.
- Learn how to engage in difficult dialogues with those who might have hurt you.
- Develop an awareness of your feelings and all emotions.
- Use your feelings and emotions as methods for story-writing and finding your voice.

Introduction story/ Black queer literacy

One day, early senior year of high school, I came home after school to the place I was living—with my cousins—and found the door locked. I didn't find the door being locked strange. Somedays, the door was locked and I'd just use my key. Unlock the door. And boom. Enter.

Home.

However, that day, after a number of attempts, my key was not working. I kept trying anyway before I suddenly realized, or began to realize at least, that the door lock was…*changed*.

I paused for a second.

No. I say to myself.

They wouldn't lock me out.

They wouldn't change the locks.

Would they?

After convincing myself that something was wrong with the door, I walked to the curb of the apartment block and sat down. Deep in thought.

No. Not my cousins. They wouldn't do that.

I waited for someone to come home and let me in. I'm sure there was a reason for my key not working.

A brief amount of time pass. I see the family car drive by. A light blue mini-van. My family—my cousins, his wife, and their kids—were all huddled in. I look at them. They look at me. They keep going. Driving past me.

Where to?

Dinner. Or so I learned when they returned home and told me that I'd have to leave.

They kicked me out. Without notice.

They changed the locks that day while I was in school.

Without warning.

With nowhere to go, I just left. I began walking.

Somehow, I located a phone—perhaps at my then best friend Wanda's house. I called my godmother.

"You have to come and pick me up. I've been kicked out."

Within an hour, she was there to pick me up. My clothes were in a black trash bag or two.

On the drive to her place, from the South Side to the North Side of Jacksonville, I tried to explain what happened; but, despite the 20-minute drive, or so, I was not sure. I left for school that morning. The previous days were chill. Nothing seemed out of the ordinary. She was silent.

My godmother let me stay at her place for a few nights. She warned me that I could not stay long term. She had her two kids, her husband's kids, and their money was getting tight—unlike previous years, in the 1990s, where their money seemed long… you know, endless.

Anyhow—I bounced between her home and my oldest sister's, who lived on the West Side of Jacksonville. Before forcing myself into my godmother's home. To get to school, I hitched a ride with a classmate who lived around the corner in the same sub-division neighborhood as my godmother—that's until she stopped picking me up. No worries, I found the school's bus stop.

Senior year of high school and I was experiencing vast states of home/less/ness.

Without a permanent home: I couldn't practice and while I usually gave the best auditions at the beginning of the year, landing me first chair, shortly after the school year started, I lost my first chair seat. I was devastated. Music is my heart.

Oh, I play the flute. More on that latter.

———

I do not recall the reason for my being kicked out of my cousin's house—though, that was not the first time I was asked to leave. It happened frequently. Once, I was voted out by their kids.

"By show of hands, who wants him to leave," their mother asked.

They all did. After a brief stint with my dad who lived on the Northside of town, my cousin picked me back up. I sincerely think he felt bad. I was back. With them. On the Southside. Briefly.

That day though, locked out, sitting on the curb, would most certainly mark the last time I'd ever allow myself to live with them. I made sure of that. I never returned, no matter the circumstance, not during high school, and most certainly not during college.

It was only after college, and after consulting with my oldest sister, that I lived with them the summer after graduating from the University of Florida and before leaving to attend the University of Wisconsin-Madison for graduate school. I needed a place to stay, and my summer job was located on the Southside of town, very near where my cousins purchased their first home. They'd let me borrow one of their cars and assured me that this time my living with them would be better. And it was! Though, secretly, I was terrified and performed my ass off—being kind, polite, but ready to leave if I'd be kicked out.

What started out as happy times with my cousins turned out to be a living environment that was toxic, traumatic, and sad.

Shortly after I started high school, and certainly by my sophomore year, they invited me to live in their home. They sought to provide me more stable living. They, but mostly my cousin's wife, worked with my father to ensure I'd received my social security checks, SSI checks. After sometime, they began rationing my check, giving me an allowance of my own money before they completely stopped giving me my money. Instead, they used my SSI check to pay some of their house-hold bills. Talk about theft.

That day, as I sat on the curb watching them pass, my heart raged—and did so for years. As my heart raged, I began to remember my dreams. "Just make it out. Just go to college."

Inner City Sissy is my story. Far beyond just going to college and coming of age over the years in and out of the inner-city, I offer a literacy story, and particularly, a Black queer literacy story. My theory of Black queer literacy is influenced by the scholar and educator Eric Darnell Prichard. In his book, *Fashioning Lives: Black Queers and the Politics of Literacy*, Pritchard details various strategies that Black queer folk create to survive and, in so doing, define themselves against systems designed to entrench and harm them. Black queer literacy is particularly adaptive, flexible, freeing, and ultimately unique—every Black queer person survives differently.

So, what do I mean by Black queer literacy? In short, I mean learning how to:

- Love myself and navigate the world's cruelty and pleasures just as I am: a Black gay man.
- Live as a joyous, happy, fierce Black gay man, sometimes against my will and in many ways deliberately.
- Live Black Queer and Free.

In short, I have learned to love myself and to use that love as a tool to navigate the world just as I am, a Black gay man.

Indeed, through love, I've learned how to live Black Queer and Free. No longer bogged down by how the world sees me, no longer hampered by a past riddled in violence, poverty, neglect, and uncompromising disgust.

In sharing my story, I also hope to offer you, dear reader, critical analyses into the ways that my identities as a Black gay man from the south gets entangled in bias and how these strategies liberated me from these entanglements. Anti-Black racism and homophobia continue to harm people and create us versus them mentalities. Anti-Black racism and homophobia, among other forms of oppression—sexism, transphobia, ableism, xenophobia, etc.—continue to harden those against the beauty of diversity and the loveliness of our different experiences. Growing up poor and in the inner-city came with expectations and doubts about my literacy skills—or assumptions that teachers and professors made about my learning abilities. As a Black Queer Teacher, I teach against these evils, inviting students to come just as they are without compromise nor limitations.

At the heart of my Black queer literacy story is learning to *forgive*.

For years, I told myself that I've forgiven so many people who've hurt me; so many people who I've felt wronged me. Forgiven myself for indulging the act of vengenance to hurt those who I felt wronged me. Writing this story has helped me put love into action where I live, love, and forgive without compromise. Has helped me heal.

Black queer literacies offer an instructive, too. As a collective of words, Black queer literacies invites us to learn about racial justice and blackness; invites us to learn about what queer people endure; and the endless ways that the socially marginalized fight against systemic harm. Black queer literacies, indeed, invites us all, dear reader, to unlearn harmful, hurtful, violent thoughts and practices. It is very true—these practices happen on the street, at work, and in the classroom. This harm can be perpetrated by those we love, those we know—people we call friends, family, bosses, and teachers.

In December 2024, I celebrated my fortieth birthday, yes 40! As I age, I continue to learn. There is always, as Billy Porter sings, "more to learn." There is also more to sing about—there is reason to hear the song of our story.

As I write this story, I journey back home. To the inner-city. There, I find memories of my Black queer boyhood, where I forgot that I had such fun in the neighborhoods that many deemed dangerous. I reclaim the inner-city against the many stereotypes that exist about "the hood."

Yes, there was violence, but there were also kids trying to have fun.

I, too, sing Inner-City.

Additionally, I walk the hall-ways of the schools I attended, from elementary to high school to college—all public. I've encountered teachers, good and bad, who, for better or worse, were critical to my learning text book knowledge and knowledge to win at life.

I've encountered teachers who were racist, sexist, and homophobic.

I've also encountered teachers who believed in me, held out hope for me.

Helped me find the sounds of my own song.

Indeed, there is music in the inner-city, and I carry this music with me.

There is also wonder and imagination all of which helped me survive and become me. There are books, lots of books. Books by Black queer writers that saved me when, while learning as a Black queer boy/ man/ scholar, I wanted to give up. Scream. Throw it all away. The words of Black queer wrtiers, too, sang to me. Saved me.

At the very core, center, of this story, this song, is forgiving my mother whose actions have had profound consequences on my life. A reason, in part, why I was left on the curb that day outside of my cousin's apartment.

Forgiving my mother is for me the greatest love. Loving her all over again was no small feat—I've written myself into loving her ever so deeply. I offer a piece of this love through one of the hardest but most important conversations I've had in my life: talking to my mother about her abandoning her kids.

With my mother beside me, with our conversation rooted in our hearts, I found love in myself and I love this/self, deeply.

Read on.

Part I
The inner city

Figure 1 Blue Front Store, 34th & Moncrief. Jacksonville, Florida. Picture taken 2021.

1
Home/ Faggot

baby.

i have learned it

aint like they say

in the newspapers

—Sonia Sanchez[1]

1. Faggot

Faggot faggot faggotafagotfaggotfaagooootfaaaaaagggg...ot.

No matter how old I get, this word haunts me, follows me into stores, walks alongside me on the streets sometimes as a shadow and sometimes as whole people. Follows me to work, writes itself all over the walls, strikes the keyboard, inks itself on printing paper, and laughs back at me on my worst days. It terrorizes me in my dreams, where I'm running, always running away from voices, sticks, and stones breaking all my bones. It's inescapable. Ghostly. Hunting.

You see, I'm an effeminate Black gay man and growing up, I was mocked for my feminine ways, or as they said "acting like a girl." Everyone, everywhere, had something to say about me and faggot was that something they said. Always.

"Boy you sound like a girl. Lil faggot"

"Boy you talk like a girl. Faggot ass"

"Boy you walk like a girl. Faggot"

"Boy, you run like a girl. Black ass faggot"

When faggot did not fall from their mouths, other words did.

"Nigga get that arch out your back"

"Boy stop hanging around all these girls."

"You ain't nothing but a lil sissy.

Faggot ass nigga.

As a little Black boy, I had no time to be little. No time to be innocent. No time to be cute. No time to just be.

Often I cried.

As I cried, I wished those who hurled these words at me would just leave me alone.

As I cried, I never understood why I could not be just like the other boys. Mitchell, in particular, was one such boy. Everyone loved him. But he, and his fat cousin, bullied me. Beat me up, cornered me behind buildings, or just followed me home, and—

"You ain't nothing but a lil sissy."

"Hit'em, Mitchell. Hit'em. Beat dat nigga ass"

He did. Often.

As always, I ran home crying. Crying. Running up the steps to my mother. Crying.

All she could do was hold me.

"What's the matter, June Bug? Tell momma what happened."

Through sniffles and tears and more crying, I told my mother what happened.

She would hold me fiercely, rock me. Hold me. Rock me. Until I slept. Slept for hours in my mother's arms.

2. The joy of stealing shit

I grew up in the inner-city, what many called "the ghetto." Everyone in the many neighborhoods I lived in throughout various sides of towns in Jacksonville, Florida was, for the most part, poor or very poor working class. Everyone was Black. Everyone struggled. Everyone knew everyone.

My mother received food stamps and spent much of her life working at hotels as a Maid.

La Quinta Inn.

My mother worked at La Quinta when I was in kindergarten. She loved that job, and I loved going to work with her on days I didn't attend school. She was good at that job. She always made beds perfectly and folded the sheets perfectly. After years of bending over in the service of labor, she now has back issues and needs a walker to assist with her mobility. Though she yearns to work, she can't.

My mother was also on drugs. She smoked crack, drank alcohol, and did the best she could as a single-mother to provide for the five of her six kids, who all lived with her in homes that usually had one bathroom and three bedrooms. The girls shared a room, and the boys shared a room. She shared a room with her then-boyfriend, Frank. To this day, I want to kill him.

Drugs. There were a lot of drugs in the community. My mother was not alone in her addiction. The streets were filled with people who sought to escape the harsh realities that resulted from underresourced communities and politicians who did not care. Police officers on the hunt for us all.

Drug dealers, too, walked the streets. They were, for the most part, very kind—and very sexy! Tattoos, muscles, dimples, brown eyes. Grey eyes. Green eyes. Chocolate skin. Caramel skin. Redbones, yellow bones. Tall. Short. Bow-legged. Gold teeth, silver chain necklaces, Jodeci Boots—this was the 90s after all. The 1990s.

They spoke when spoken to. "What's up shawty." "Yo, lemme holla at you." And when you did not speak, they called you out. "Oh, so you don't see me?" You too good to speak today? Aiight then. Bitch ass, nigga. Be like that."

In my early teens, I discovered that sweet sticky stuff they possessed between their legs and that they only shared late at night. "Hey let me holla at you" carried different meanings after dark when I got a little taller, and when my body was changing from lil faggot boy to teen-boy, fuckable faggot. "Let me show you something." "You like that." "I see the way you be lookin' at me."

Takes off his shirt.

"You like what you see?" "Do this." "Harder. Up and down. Harder. Faster." Shiiitttt. (deep breath).

"Eh, don't tell no body. Sexy ass. Here, take this. Don't spend it all in one place."

They even gave us kids a dollar or two to buy cookies from the corner store, or the "candy lady" who usually lived with her "sister." Now-and-Laters (or as I often pronounced these in one breath: "nowanlateahs"). And juicies and boxed candies, 25 cents. Pickles, 50 cents. Pig-feet, 75 cents. Jar Heads, Johnny Apple-Seeds, Lemon Heads, Boston Baked Beans, 25 cents each. From the Candy lady: Lemon cookies. Strawberry cookies. Chocolate chip cookies that we often wore as rings on our fingers—10 cents a bag or 15 cookies for 25 cents.

Blue Front was my favorite corner store—and the most popular among those who lived in Palm Terrace—off "34th and Moncrief." I stole so much from Blue Front. I tucked stuff in my front pants, clearly believing that the cashier didn't see this huge bulge in my pants. With food stamps given to me by my mother, I bought so much stuff, too—so I stole a lil bit bought a lil bit! "Junior, run to the store and get…"

Whenever we needed one or two items—eggs, butter, bread—I, either alone or with my sister, Dee Dee, would run down the street to Blue Front. To buy and steal and sometimes curse the cashier out—usually the owner—for accusing us of stealing. "You lying. I ain't steal shit, mother fucker." But I did. Always. He wasn't lying. Even at the age of less than 10, I cursed like a sailor.

I had so much fun stealing.

3. Bethune Elementary

I also had fun at the Boys and Girls Club. You see. So many folks give the hood, the inner-city, a bad rep.

Crime infested

Drug infested
Roach infested

Black on Black Crime.
Welfare mothers
Absent father
Lazy Niggers
Dirty ass kids

Bad schools
Horrible teachers

Figure 2 Main Entrance. Mary McLeod Bethune Elementary School.
Picture taken December 27, 2024.

Those are lies they told you. The lies that many politicians tell themselves to maintain white supremacy, manifest white-savior syndrome, and perpetuate the lie of Black depravity.

Don't get it twisted—the hood is distinct. There were drugs. We had roaches. There were lots of fights. People got shot. Some killed. There were single mothers, single fathers, wayward parents.

Many schools were underfunded. Many lacked resources. Graffiti art decorated the exterior of buildings.

But we are not dumb, or stupid. Or lazy. We had fun. We expressed our genius through song, dance, and artistry of various kinds—including graffiti and tagging.

Dance:

> "The Butterfly uh uh that's old let me see the tootsie roll!"[2]

Play:

> Jig-a low
> jigjig aloow
> Yo, Quita,
> yo?
> Are you ready?
> For what
> To jig
> Jig what
> Jiga low

Figure 3 My Kindergarten class was located down this wing of the School. Mary McLeod Bethune Elementary School. Picture taken December 27, 2024.

Learn:

Through kindergarten and second grade, I attended Mary McLeod Bethune Elementary School—named after the Black Civil Rights activists and educator herself! And, to reiterate, I lived in Palm Terrace. I recited our address with excitement to my Kindergarten teacher, Ms McCready. She taught us to remember our address so that just in case we babies ever got lost, we could, with the help of the police, find our away home. I recited my address proudly!

4545 Moncrief Road, Apartment 24.

Palm Terrace was once a lively a multi-complex apartment housing development on the Northside of Jacksonville right around the corner from Bethune Elementary and down the street from Blue Front. However, Bethune elementary has since closed, and it was not because of stupid lazy nigger kids. Rather, it closed because the school was built on lands once dubbed, "Brown's Dump," a stretch of land along Moncrief Road, including 34th and 33rd streets, that once served as a toxic waste site for the city.[3] Between the 1940s and 1960s, the city dumped cancer-causing toxins on the grounds that became Bethune Elementary and the surrounding neighborhoods—including Palm Terrace and the general area known as Leonard Circle, which composed mostly of working-class Black families and where I would soon discover my extended family—including my eldest sister.[4]

My mother knew nothing about Brown's Dump and, I don't imagine, did school officials. We stayed in Palm Terrace for years, and I began attending Bethune in 1989. The school closed in 2001, two years before I graduated high school at Douglas Anderson School of the Arts. Clean-up efforts led and facilitated by the EPA[5] began in 2006, a year before I graduated from the University of Florida, and wrapped up in 2018, three years after I earned my doctorate from the University of Michigan. Although the school has closed, Bethune Elementary still stands, though behind a wired fence

While we lived in Palm Terrace, we were on HUD and paid next to nothing in rent. HUD, or Housing and Urban Development, is a federal program that helps low-income families pay their rent or purchase homes with government vouchers. In order to qualify for HUD and their financial assistance program, a family's total income must be or exists close to the poverty-line[6]. These families, like mine, were also on food stamps and on Free-or-Reduced lunch programs. At Bethune, I ate breakfast and lunch for free. I simply loved the breakfast donut—"Sun Rise donut," it was called. When school let out, I would walk home and go straight to the Boys & Girls Club. My mother instructed me to go to the Boys & Girls Club right after school because, after all, she was at work and nobody would be home at the time of my being dismissed from school.

The best part of my childhood is, in fact, the result of me going their daily. The Boys and Girls Club was so central to my laughter and literacy development.

Figure 4 4545, Moncrief Road. Apt 24. Palm Terrace Apartments. We lived in the upper right-hand corner. The Boys & Girls Club was down stairs to the left. Picture taken December 27, 2024.

4. The Boys and Girls Club

The Boys & Girls Club, what we simply called "the club," was located downstairs from my apartment in Palm Terrace. Literally, my sisters, brothers, and I were always the first people at the club. The club's Director was Mr Johnson—who everyone affectionally called "Mr J." Mr J loved me and my family. He was also the first Black Educator in my life and somehow felt like a god-father to us all. Though my sister, Devita—aka "Dee Dee"—was and, to this day, remains his absolute favorite. She's lovely.

At the club, I developed a penchant for playing regular, "8-cubed" pool and bumper pool. Whenever Mr J opened the door, everyone rushed to the back of the club to the pool table, only to find that I was already there, having first dibs on the pool stick and first round of play. I mean I was good and won several of the low-stakes tournaments.

I also enjoyed foosball, you know, the game that looks like soccer and that you control by moving the attached sticks. I was always the "goalie" and would strike the ball with such force and thus score many points. I defended well.

What I loved most, however, was the brain brawl tournaments and the track meets. During brain-brawl tournaments, Mr J introduced us to many "Black firsts" and posted placards with their picture and a brief bio of their life and accomplishments along the walls of the club. At any point, from any position in the club, you could read about Jackie Robinson, Jackie-Joyner Kersee, Thurgood Marshall, Daniel Hale Williams, Garret Morgan, James Weldon Johnson, Booker T. Washington, George Washington

Carver, Martin Luther King Jr., Mahalia Jackson, Marian Anderson, and yes, Mary McLeod Bethune—since many, if not all of us in the club, attended Bethune elementary.

Many of us attended the club after school. If we did not have homework after school, then we were required to read through these biographies before playing pool or any games.

Mr Johnson, along with, Mrs Williams—whose official title eludes me but who often served as the club's unofficial no-nonsense Associate Director and beloved godmother—worked at the club for years. Collectively, they introduced us to U.S. States and their capitals. Club tournaments always quizzed us on states and their capitals. I did well, mostly, but the winner always—always!—was my sister, Devita. That girl knew her states and capitals!

But track, that was me! I was fast. Usually, the fastest in my age group, boys 12 and under. My sister Devita was fast, too, but Shameka Williams—Mrs Williams' daughter—was the fastest girl at the club. She was one of the fastest girls in the city. No one, and I mean nobody, ever beat her. I wanted so much to run like her, win as much as she did.

In the summer, the Boys and Girls Club hosted track and field competitions between the clubs throughout the city and the winning clubs—the top two or three in each city—competed across the state. Shameka always won. My sister, Devita, won in her division, too. I could never start as fast, and often came in second—but I did win a few! I don't know if it was me or the gun, but I always heard the gun moments after the referee shot it. Then I'd take off and have to catch up to the pack of fast boys— who I thought were, in fact, really slow!

Beyond winning track meets, we all supported each other and created bonds at the club. Clubs across the city hated us and we relished being the favorites each summer. I mean, nobody could beat us. Perhaps our biggest threat was "the Romona girls." Now *they* were fast!

But more than anything, I believe the other clubs hated our sense of family, created and maintained by Mr J and Mrs Williams.

When Mr J left the Palm Terrace branch of the Boys and Girls Club to serve as the Director for the Romona Branch, he took us all with him, and yep, even there we became an unstoppable force. Whenever Mr J left to lead various branches, we simply followed—Ocean Way, Durkeeville, Brentwood. Again, we loved him. Our beloved community god-father.

Because I learned so much from the Boys and Girls Club, I often excelled at school. Somehow, I just understood that being the best, the smartest, was important—either for trophies or academic awards. In short, school was never an issue for me because in the ghetto I was fortunate enough to have a Boys and Girls Club led by two Black people, Mr J and Mrs Williams; they loved us fiercely. Because of them, I could read just fine, write just fine, and do math just fine. Occasionally, my bad attitude earned me low marks in citizenship. Back then, in the early 1990s, teachers gave grades in citizenship and those grades were based on behavior and how much a teacher liked, or disliked, me. Outside of that, I was often on the honor-roll, along with my sister, Devita. She got straight "A's" in citizenship. Always. Her teachers, up until about fifth grade, loved her. After puberty, she became very pretty and a defiant menace. A girl from the hood, with sass and ghetto fabulousness: brains, beauty, glam, and ready to kick your ass if you bothered her little sissy brother—me.

We were brainiacs, really. We both loved school. We are our mother's two youngest children, and we clung to each other throughout our childhood. Even now, as adults, we are pretty inseparable. Now, I'd kick anyone's ass if they so as breathed heavy on her.

But our love for each other, us inner-city Black kids at the club, don't often make sensational news headlines. We were simply Black, poor, and under developed.

Lies.

We were a loving, kind, a street family. Trophy snatchers. Fast as hell.

Fast.

As.

Hell.

"You lying. I ain't steal shit, mother fucker."

"Kick his faggot ass."

5. The day I kicked his ass

"Lissen baby," my mother would always say after I'd wake up from my sleeping in her arms. "You gonna have to fight them boys back. Momma not always gone be here to protect you."

My mother, Angel Girl, is short. She, at the time, had long beautiful black hair that she would spend considerable time styling before work or walking me to school. She, like me, has dark skin, and everyone always told my momma that she was beautiful.

Chocolate beauty. At the time, when we lived in Palm Terrace, she was around 26 or 28, certainly not 30. Yes, at this young age in her life, she had already had six kids. She had her first child, my older brother, at age 14.

At age 26 or 28, my mother had a mouth on her and could curse—or as we say, "cuss"—up a storm. People say I get my attitude from her—I can see it. My mother is nice until she's had enough of your ass, or you have worked her last nerve. I'm the same way.

Anyhoot—my mom always went to Mitchell's house, or anyone who would bully me—and gave them a piece of her gawt-damn mind. Always.

Afterward, or before, she would talk to me and tell me that I would have to stand up for myself. Her tender conversations were important lessons crucial to me surviving those tough Palm Terrace streets.

"If they hit you, hit them back."

She also told me to use the closest anything as a weapon. Book or brick.

"Once you fight back and beat his ass, he will leave you alone."

I soon discovered that she was right.

Mitchell hardly attended the club. Whenever he came, he would cause so much trouble. He disrespected everyone. Ms Williams was never having any of his foolishness. She, or Mr Johnson, often threw him out of the club and suspended him for days. Yes, you could be banned from the clubs for days if not weeks.

I would later discover that Mitchell, like most of us, was suffering from what we all suffered from—being Black in the inner-city.

His dad sold drugs. His mother was young and wayward: here and there, but never *there*. His fat cousin was, it seemed all he had. Mitchel was angry. *All. the. time.* We were the same age. A young angry 12 and under boy who barely lived in the world, but yet, had already absorbed all the hatred that world had of him—brown dumps, sites of waste killing Black bodies.

He spewed that hatred back on me. An inner-city sissy just trying to win at track, in Brain brawl tournaments, and enjoy Sun Rise donuts in a cafeteria whose school I had no idea was built on a toxic waste site. An inner-city Black boy with no consciousness to fight back at life, be it striking back at him or confronting racist politicians who reduced my communities to waste. I was only a kid!

"Kick his ass, Mitchell."

The day that I fought Mitchell back, and kicked his ass, is the day I understood that this was just the beginning. As an effeminate Black gay man, as an inner-city sissy, I would have to fight not only for my survival but also for those like me and I would have to do so in the name of love and yes, resistance.

My mom was right, Mitchell never bothered me again.

I kicked his gawtdamn ass.

And I never saw him again.

We soon moved out of Palm Terrace. Out of Brown's Dump.

Shit, however, would soon hit the fan, and it would be the last time I'd ever see my mother as beautiful. The last time I'd feel the security of home. The last time I'd witness my mother curling and styling her long black hair for hours.

Crack nearly ate her alive.

Part II
Mother

2
Prelude/ Memory

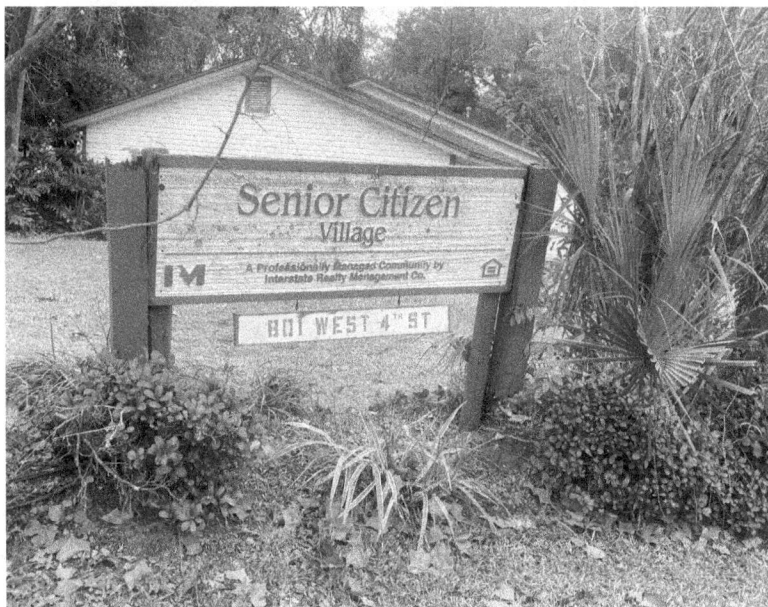

Figure 5 Senior Citizen Village, where my grandfather lived. Picture taken December 26, 2024.

One morning, mid-to-late summer of August 1994, and shortly before I was to start the fourth grade, my mother, Angel Girl, left for the local Pic-n-Save store and…*did not return home until nearly three years later.*

The morning was typical. I was lying on the floor of my grandfather's living room—doing what, I don't quite remember. Though, I'm sure I was thinking about school. I loved school, especially the first days of school. My grandfather, Eddie, was more than likely sitting in his chair at his infamous, wooden, weatherworn, yet sturdy cards table. He was either playing solitaire—with actual cards—or imagining, I reckon, his winning strategies for whenever he would assemble family and friends over for a rousing game of spades. My grandfather was a consummate spades player—and he loved minor league baseball, too. He and I regularly attended games of the Jacksonville Suns, the city's then Minor League baseball team.

Anyhoot—

My mother, his only child, was busying herself in the bathroom. Getting dressed, doing her hair, moving about the small one-bedroom home located in the "new" Blodget homes for senior citizens. We often stayed at my grandfather's, making residential space within his tiny one-bedroom apartment. Funny thing? My mother had an apartment in a place called Flag Street Apartments, but we were hardly there. We stayed with grandaddy so much that one day, out of the blue, we returned to the Flag Street apartment to a home infested by funk! All of the food and milk had spoiled. The stench of forgotten trash mixed the air with the smell of dirty laundry that lined the walls in just about every room of a three-bedroom apartment. My nose began to bleed!

Nevertheless, finally dressed, my mother said something to grandaddy before approaching me with her always affectionate motherly love.

"Junior," I was named after my daddy, "momma finna run to the store."

Although she would usually take me along with her, on this day she did not.

"Can I come momma?"

"No, but momma gonna bring you back some stuff for school."

"Please, momma?"

"No baby. Stay here with your grandaddy."

Figure 6 The apartment my grandfather lived. Picture taken December 26, 2024.

Perhaps I cried, perhaps I pouted. I'm sure I reacted in the way the youngest spoiled child typically responded when being told, "no." The youngest spoiled child who was always with his momma.

Whatever transpired in those moments ended with me telling my mother what I wanted for school: a Sonic the Hedgehog trapper keeper.

"Momma, can you get me the Sonic the Hedgehog trapper keeper?"

"Yes, baby. Momma will get you that."

And with that, momma was gone.

I went back to doing whatever I was doing. But this time, I was excited, giddy even, at the idea of having what was then a popular and in-demand school item—a trapper keeper. And not just any ole one, a Sonic the Hedgehog one.

As the day went on, hours passed and I wondered when momma was getting back. She walked to the Pic-N-Save before, which is quite the hike, so I knew that she could be gone for hours. I knew the distance because she and I walked there plenty enough times from my grandfather's house. We would walk from Jefferson Street, all the way to Main and 1st Street, where Pic-N-Save was located.

Evening set on the day. There was still no momma.

By that afternoon, I began walking from my grandfather's apartment, located in the back of the Senior Citizen's village community, way to the front. I'd sit at the entrance and wait to see if my mother was coming. I'd sit for an hour, then go back to my grandfather's apartment for a bit—to pee probably and grab somethin' to eat or check on him—before heading back to the corner to sit. I'd even walk up the street a bit, to the corner of the Jefferson Street pool, with the hopes of walking into my mother.

Figure 7 4th & Madison, the corner of the Senior Citizens Village where I sat waiting for my mother. Picture taken December 26, 2024.

Nothin'.

I stayed at the entrance for so long—sitting, standing, looking— that the guard and people in the front office, and on-lookers, began to wonder.

"You okay, baby?"

"Yeah, I'm fine."

"You Eddie's baby—yo grandaddy know you down here?"

"Yeah, he home."

By the second sunset, you know, my mother had still not returned.

I went to sleep that night worried.

The next day, was like déjà vu: I stood, sat, sat and stood, at the entrance of the community.

Waiting

Looking.

Walking

Sitting.

Sunset again.

No mother.

Nightfall.

No mother.

Next morning.

"Grandaddy, have you seen momma?"

I don't recall my grandfather saying much—and he wasn't a man of few words!

He either looked worried or not surprised at all.

I visited the corner for a few more days before realizing…

"All at once"…that

Momma was…

gone.[7]

———

Seemingly, my mother had abandoned her kids. Left us for some no-count man. At least, this is the narrative that I'd learned from overhearing adults speak about my mother. She was called every name left of Satan. None of which I care to rehearse here.

In many ways, as I began to grow up, come of age, and experience life motherless, no other rumor impacted me more than this one: that my mother didn't love her kids. That she loved herself, the drugs that she was on, and that no-count man, much more. I struggled mightily with the possible truth that my mother, the woman who brought me into this world, did not love me; that she did not love her kids. I believed the rumor and struggled… believed and struggled…believed and struggled…Until now.

The next series of chapters is the conversation of my life—a long conversation that I had with my mother about her decision to leave and abandon her children. A decision, in fact, that knots together pieces of my life, heart, and the world I've since had to navigate without her. This is a conversation of reckoning, of accountability and, ultimately, one of healing.

In small pieces, before speaking with my mom, interviewing her, we've had such a conversation. The difference here is that I've grown past the rage that I specifically reserved for her and unleashed whenever I could. The difference now is one, well I'm much older, and two the desire to understand and see my mother in humanizing ways; her flaws and all.

Yes, while the principle question that I needed to answer concerns her decision to leave, while speaking with my mother, I got a chance, finally, and perhaps for the first time, to get to know her *for her*—discover her story. I listened to tales of her own becoming, her own Black girlhood; how she experienced the inner-city; how she found and experienced love; and most importantly, how she survived three decades of smoking crack, and living with men who beat her. She's a survivor on multiple fronts.

Loving my mother, again, was not easy, and there are days when the past haunts me and I want to cry all over again. I'm human and still healing. Yet, on these days I extend myself grace and trust that love is a process and requires time, commitment, and belief.

The conversations over the next chapter detail my mother's girlhood, her becoming a mother, and ultimately her surviving drugs and domestic violence, and her returning home to her children.

3
Angel Girl/ Motherhood

My mother, Angela Danise Dean-Green, was born on February 24, 1961, in Jacksonville, Florida. She is the only child between Hattie Mae Dean and Eddie Dean—my grandparents. Until she was 11 years old, she was raised mostly by her grandmother, whose name is also Hattie Green. Her father, my grandaddy Eddie, who affectionately referred to my mother as "Angel Girl," provided for her tremendously and well into her adult years. My mother had six children and had her first child at age 14. She dropped out of school by tenth grade. In her twenties she worked as a domestic throughout hotels in Jacksonville. She married my father, David Sr, and had four children with him. Though they never divorced, they were very, very separated.

David: **Momma, what was your first memory of when I [David] was born? When you found out that you were pregnant with me, what was going through you mind?**

Angela: Another one. [laughter]….another child.

David: **Was this pregnancy expected?**

Angela: Way unexpected. You was way unexpected.

David: **Were you expecting any of your children?**

Angela: [long pause] No.

David: **So, you were out there having relations with men and getting pregnant?**

Angela: No. [Laughter]

David: **When you were pregnant with me or anyone else, were you happy, were you distraught, were you like what I'm gonna do? I'm too young for this… I don't wanna be a mom. Or where you like I'm excited? Or…What were your emotions like?**

Angela: When I got pregnant wit'chu?

David: **Yes…or any of us really.**

Angela: Well, when I got pregnant with Darrel, I wasn't expected that at all. I was too young then

David: **How old were you?**

Angela: Fourteen [14].

David: **And you were too young…you were not expecting that.**

Angela: No. I was too young. I ain't no nothin' about raising no kids.

David: **Hmmhmm. Okay. And then what?**

Angela: Well, when I had him, I got pregnant with Ann. that's when Daddy took Darrel to his momma house. And Ann daddy took her to his momma house (I reckon).

My mother had six children. The oldest two are Darrell and Ann, whom she references above, followed by the third child, my late brother O.B. And while I did not direct our conversation there, the separation of my mother from her two eldest kids began at this time with great confusion and misunderstanding about why my grandfather took Darrel to live with his own father and why Ann was taken by her daddy to live with her grandmother. The latter, the memories surrounding Ann, and why she was taken to live with her grandmother—around the corner on Leonard Circle—is filled with hurt and pain. And while I've asked my mother about the circumstances involved in moving my sister Ann to live with her grandmother, I leave it up to them to clarify the story. I still sense that there is unprocessed pain and grief between these two, and it hurts my heart knowing that the truth still needs to be told so that if not love, then something close to it, can repair this enduring wound between them.

I tuck this narrative within the fold of my heart and allow myself back into the conversation with my mother, who, by the way, kept talking, reconfiguring the math that separates Ann and O.B in age.

David: **[So] you have your first two kids. Then sometime had passed before O.B. arrived. Six years. Then Hattie is after OB. A year later**

Angela: Yeah. Then DeeDee and then you.

David: **DeeDee and Mae Mae is three years apart?**

Angela: Yeah. Then you.

David: So, when you had me and you were thinking. This is it. I'm not having any more kids?

Angela: Yeah. I hurried up and remedied that.

After having me, my mother got her "tubes tied," as we say—a medical process formally called tubal ligation foreclosed (at least in the short term) the possibility of my mother having any more kids.

Yet, there is more to the story of why my mother got her tubes tied, which we speak about later in our conversation.

But before we get to that story of my mother's life, let me clarify some names a bit. To reiterate, "Dee Dee" is short for Devita— whose full name is Devita Danielle Green, while "Mae Mae" is the nickname version of my sister Hattie's middle name, whose full name is Hattie Mae Green.

I've always found the names of my brothers and sisters unique, if not strange, if not country as hell. I was curious so I asked my mother about our names, uncovering in part my mother's detail to the importance of linguistic ancestry. As you will see, dear reader, through naming, my mother creates and preserves lineages that archives, quite powerfully, a host of memories: memories of her own childhood and those that she attached to her own mother and father, my father and their relationships, marriage, and after-marriage life.

1. Black girlhood and love

David: Momma, how did you first meet daddy?

Angela: Through yo aunt.

David: Debora [laughter]? How did that happen?

My auntie Deborah met my dad, David Sr, when she lived off Suitel Drive in Jacksonville, Florida. They hit it off as friends and soon took a trip to Mardi Gras in Orlando, Florida. My dad often visited with my auntie Deborah and one day, while mother was out in the yard playing with Deborah's kids, my mother's nephews, she cut the bottom of her foot on a pine cone. Initially, my mother refused to go to the clinic to get her foot properly treated. However, my dad, who was at the time a stranger to my mother, insisted that she must go, and so he took her. From that moment, they soon started courting and going out and dating.

Angela: And he came out there one Friday or one Saturday or something and he told me that I was going to get my foot sew'n up. I say "well who is you?"

So he took me to the doctor…and he got my foot sew'n. And me and him was together ever since.

Almost immediately, and without me asking about the details of her relationship with my dad, my mother then starts to recount the infidelity and domestic violence she suffered from my father. The anger rose in her voice not just below but when she first mentioned my father not being there in the hospital after I was born.

Angela: I went through pru'de [trans vernacular for pure] hell with dat man

[Long pause]

Yo daddy was a trip.

David: **What made'em a trip?**

Angela: Becuz, I didn't know he had another wife. And another family.

David: **Oh (I say shockingly).**

Angela: Dis woman comin' out here to my sister [Deborah] house talkin' bout I'mma call the police. Police say to that woman ain't nothin' we can do that woman [my mom] done had two kids.

My mom clarifies that she was an adult and not a child or teen like the woman thought.

David: **Are you talking about Shirley? [Shirley is my youngest brother, Eric's mom]**

Angela: No. I'm talkin' about his wife Sadie.

David: **I don't know…I've never heard of her…Sadie?**

Angela: I know it

David: **Sadie…who is? This is some high drama [as I say this my momma is laughing]. So are you saying … my daddy, your husband…He was considerably older than you [lost train of thought because I was so shocked at this news of Sadie]. How old were you at the time?**

Angela: I was seventeen…eighteen.

David: **And how old was daddy?**

Angela: I think he was in his thirties.

David: Oh gosh…And so, he had already had a wife named Sadie and had children?

Angela: Yes.

David: What was his children's names? Do you know the children?

Angela: One of them was named…I can't think of the boy name. The girl name hmm.. I can't think of neither one of the girls names right now…hmmm

David: It's okay momma

Angela: One of them was staying with me and him. And I think that was the baby girl. And she mess round here and when out there and got pregnant.

David: Oh okay… So, you met daddy under the circumstances of you going to the doctor.

    This is how y'all fell in love [and] got married. How quick did you start dating?

    Did you date first? Or did you get married first? And what year was that?

Angela: We dated and stayed together for a while. We got married…[pause]

    Let me see. I got the marriage license. The day we got married Mae Mae started walkin'.

David: So, you got married after you had kids with daddy?

Angela: Hmmhmm.

David: Do you know what year that was?

Angela: Mae Mae was born in '80…that was '81.

In short, my mother and father were married in 1981, the day my sister Hattie "Mae Mae" began walking.

My sister Hattie holds such symbolic memory for my mother. As evidenced in my mother's memory, she could only remember the year she married my daddy by remembering the exact day and year that my sister Mae Mae began walking.

Yet, my mother named Hattie after both her own mother and her grandmother. Both of their names were Hattie. More intriguing here is that my sister Hattie was born on the day that my mother's mother, grandmother Hattie, died—which was on Mother's Day, May 11, 1980.

My mother's memory is at best uneven throughout the interview. Some aspects of her past she remembers hazily. However, through the names of her children, she can unlock memories with exacting precision. My brother O.B. was named after my paternal grandfather because as my mother remembers, my father was adamant that he wanted their first son to have his own father's name. My mother changed the spelling from Obie, to simply O.B.

Sitting alone one day, my mother began saying the name Da-vee-ta. And she

thought the named sounded beautiful, and thus gifted this name to her last

daughter, Devita. She thought the name was beautiful because it closely resembled

my father's. I'm of course named after my father.

The name "Hattie" led to a conversation with my mother about her own childhood and relationship with her own mother.

David: **What was your childhood like? [I know you had auntie Deborah] Did you grow up in Jacksonville?**

Angela: Yes, that's my home.

David: **Yeah. And you had granddaddy [Eddie]?**

Angela: I had my grandmama. She lived on the Westside.

David: **So, you grew up with your grandmother? What was her name? Was Mae Mae named after grandmamma Hattie?**

Angela: Yeah. She was named after my mamma and my grand-mamma. My momma and my grandmamma had the same name

David: **So, Mae Mae is named after both your mother and your grandmother, so our great grand grandmother?**

Angela: Hmmhmm.

David: **Granddaddy didn't raise you. But your grandmother did?**

Angela: Yeah.

David: **Where was you mother?**

Angela: My momma was an alcoholic… she died from sclero-sis of the liver when I was seven years old.

David: **So that means that she was not around a lot?**

Angela: No [coughs] My grandmother came and got me.

David: **What made your grandmother come and get you from her?**

Angela: Because I wasn't been fed.

My daddy…stayed.. daddy on…

At this point, my mother begins to speak quickly—and to the point that I could not understand her. So, I asked her to repeat herself so that I could hear her discuss her daddy, my grandaddy, not being around a lot… because he worked a lot. I sense, from her quickened speech, that my mother's memories begin unlocking the trauma she experienced as a child, so I proceed cautiously.

David: **Hold on momma. Where did granddaddy work?**

Angela: …[pause] he worked at Sea-bo Wine Company.

David: **Oh, I didn't know that. So, granddaddy worked at a Wine company? What did he do there?**

Angela: Every store he went to was on David street-- that's where he delivered wine at.

David: **Oh he delivered wine!!**

Angela: Hmmhmm.

David: **How amazing. I didn't know that. I wish I had'a known. [we both laugh]**

So, then I clarify. My mother was not being fed by her own mother, so great grandmother Hattie, my mother's grandmother, came and got her and began to raise her. My mother agrees with my understanding of her story/ memory.

David: How long did she [Great Grandmother Hattie] raise you?

Angela: She raised me until…until…what I got eleven…and I went to go stay with my daddy.

David: Granddaddy? So, grandaddy took you from there?

My mother didn't answer this question, instead, continues by recalling the death of her grandmother—a conversational detail not provoked by any question.

Angela: She died…when we stayed over there on 3rd and Walnut [Long pause].

That's when she died.

David: What did she die from?

Angela: I reckon a heart attack. When they came and got me …I went out there to St. Vincent. I was holding her hand when she died.

David: Oh Jesus. [I say with utter shock].

Angela: They were looking for daddy [my mother's daddy, Eddie]. Couldn't find him. We finally found him.

I don't ask or say much else related to the death of either my mother's mother or her grandmother. The image of a young Black girl holding her grandmother's hand, the one woman who took care of her when hardly anyone else did or cared to, hurts my heart.

Listening closely to the timbre of my mother's voice, I sense that the death of her grandmother continues to shake her, especially since the cause of her death was not clear to her. She "reckons" that her grandmother died of a heart attack. In the South, when folks use "reckon" to describe something or someone, it means that they are not sure; they either assume or believe from their intuition. Yet, the lack of details surrounding the death of a Black woman speaks to the long history of how hospitals have unfairly, unethically, and, in many cases, violently treated Black women.

Nevertheless, my mother spoke rather evenly of this moment, wryly in fact. Her non-emotional voice seems to repress any hurt, though I sense the hurt within her—and the refusal to tap into the hurt. A saddened hurt 7-year-old Angel Girl and the now 63-year-old adult Angela still carries with her the grief that comes with the loss of a mother.

Thus, in naming my sister Hattie, my mother remembers her own mother and grandmother. These are not easy memories. However, they stand as memories that she can retrieve when she needs them most and tucks them away when their weight becomes too heavy a burden. Memories of her mother and grandmother live in a name passed down through time.

In this context, I wondered if my mom's choice to carry forth the name Hattie was born out of the love she had for her mother and grandmother. My mother loved her mother and grandmother fiercely. However, when asked, my mother could not recall a time when her own mother told her that she loved her.

In this way, I asked my mother about her childhood, her parents, and about feeling love from them.

David: **How would you describe grandaddy? Was he other than just a man who worked... Was, like, he out in**

the street partying? Was he, like, a trollop? Was he, like, a man whore? Was he loving? What was he like?

Angela: Daddy was a hoe.

David: Granddaddy? (I say shockingly).

Angela: Your grandaddy was a hoe. I'mma tell you dat now.

David: [I laugh hysterically] Why you say that?

Angela: Because he was.

After learning that my Granddaddy was a "hoe," I also learned from my mother that he served as a cook in the United States Army.

David: So, granddaddy was in the Army. He raised you. What was life for you growing up with grandaddy? What was it like for little Angela growing up?

Angela: Well, little Angela thought she was grown. That's what lil Angela thought.

Cuz when I got tired of Daddy. I would go to Deborah house. Cuz there this one woman he was going with, Betsy, me and her couldn't get along at all. She talkin bout, well I'm your step momma. Nah you step the hell. Cuz I aint had nothing but one momma and she dead and gone. Cuz I ain't believe in that step momma nothin.

David: [light chuckle from me] Momma, when you say you thought you were grown… What does that mean for you momma?

Angela: Because I felt like I was on my own.

[long pause]

> The only time I seen my daddy…. When I was staying with my grandmamma I would see my daddy every week cuz he would come out [there] and give my grandma some money every week. He would come out there on his lunch break every week on that wine truck and [I] would go down there and meet'em. He took care of me when I was with my grandmomma. He made sure of that every week.

David: **I love granddaddy.**

Angela: But when it came to ya'll. Hhnnhhh, nooo bbbbaby. I ain't have to worry about buying no clothes. He bought ya'll Christmas every year.

My mother was right about that, my granddaddy spoiled us all, especially me!

David: **Now momma, at any point did you feel that your parents (daddy or momma) loved you at all?**

Angela: I knew my daddy loved-ed me. And I kinda felt like my momma loved me. But she couldn't take care of me. She was sick. The last time I seen my momma. I had ran away …we went to church one Sunday. I wanted to see my momma. Grandma told me I couldn't see her. I left the church. I…walked all the way down Myrtle Avenue. To where my momma stayed at. And that's the day she went to the hospital.

David: **Wait a minute go back momma. You were at church?**

Angela: Yeah

David: **What church were you at?**

Angela: Westside Church of Christ right dere on McCoy Blvd.

David: **Is it still there?**

Angela: No. It was a lil o lil bitty like Pink and White church and it just sat right there off the express way.

David: **So, you walked from there?**

Angela: From all the way from there. And walked under the Under Pass (highway) all the way down Myrtle Avenue to my momma because I wanted to see my momma. And that's the day she went to the hospital.

David: **[After gathering my shock and lost of words] You were seven years old when she died?**

Angela: Hmmhmm. Yep.

David: **And you walked all the way down Myrtle Avenue at seven?**

Angela: Yep

David: **And in that time period, when you were seven years old, did you mother ever tell you that she loved you? Did you feel that she loved you? Or there was no sense of that…it was just that this is just my daughter?**

Angela: I can't remember all that. But I know the day I went to go see my momma they had to call the ambulance to come and get her.

David: **Did you love your mother?**

Initially, I don't think that my mother heard this question because after she shared that the ambulance came to get her mother, she discussed that someone was living downstairs.

Angela: Deborah was staying right down stairs…in the Rooming House[8] still there off Myrtle Avenue.

David: **[I then repeat:] Momma did you love your mother?**

Angela: Yes. [she says emphatically]

David: **Because you walked all the way. You were just a walking lil child.**

Angela: Hmm…that's why my legs are like they is now.

David: **You loved your mother. Did you have any brothers or sisters?**

Angela: I had one brother. [pause]. And he got kilt.

As I replay this portion of the conversation, I began to process a pattern of emotional stillness that emerged whenever my mother spoke so exacting of death.

Here in this moment, she goes on to speak about her only brother, Ronald. Ronald was murdered by a woman. She killed him with an ice-pic, stabbing him seventeen times. As I listened to my mother recall this memory, I did not hear pain in her voice, nor sadness. The memory fell so easily from her tongue.

Considerable time elapsed in the interview before I realized that my mother had, over the years, affected performing what historian Darlene Clarke Hine calls the "culture of dissemblance." My mother had in fact shielded her inner-self, and outer-self, against the pain and grief of death—including the bloody murder of her only brother. She, on all accounts, seemed fine. The ease with which she mentions these deaths belies a woman hurt and weighed down by unprocessed grief. These conditions sit so deep within her that she's learned to carry their weight with psychological and performative ease.

Angela: As a matter fact he got kilt on in '75 [i.e. 1975]… because I was pregnant with Darrell.

David: Jesus that seems like years ago.

Angela: Yeah, that was 42 years ago.

Remember, my mother had Darrell, her first-born and my eldest sibling, when she was 14 years old. This memory of violence, and the murder of her brother, has lived in her for forty-two years.

2. A taste of the free life

To reiterate, my mom had her first child at age 14. She was in middle school at the time. At this point, I asked my mom about school. She made the decision to drop out of school, which led to consequences that ultimately steered her to drinking, smoking, engaging in criminal activity, and meeting that man who introduced her to crack cocaine.

David: Now, did you go to school when you were growing up?

Angela: Yeah, I went all the way to the what… tenth grade.

David: Tenth grade?

Angela: Yeah.

David: And what school was that?

Angela: Last school…Jeff Davis.

David: **In tenth grade?**

Angela: Hmmhmm

David: **Must have been a high school before it was a middle school.**

Angela: Yep.

David: **Now why did you stop going to school?**

Angela: [long silence] Just got bored in school…just got bored.

David: **[Laughs] Were you bored because you felt you were not being challenged by the class work… school work? What made you get bored?**

Angela: I just…

David: **Did you not like school?**

Angela: I just got bored going to school. Especially Jeff Davis.

David: **Did you have a favorite subject in school?**

Angela: Yeah.

David: **What was your favorite subject?**

Angela: Science

David: Oh really. Well, that makes a lot of sense. I love science, too!

My mother was rather uninspired by these questions, and I sensed that she wanted to move on. Clearly, something about school and Jeff Davis remains uninteresting for her, so I listened to the mood and moved on…slightly.

David: **So, you just got bored and just stopped going to school. Of course, you didn't have parents to**

reinforce the importance of going to school so you were like listen this ain't it?

Angela: Yeah. Then I went to drinking…

My mother freely, and energetically, segued into her excursion into the world of drinking!

David: So, what year was that? Was it tenth grade for you?

Angela: I was sixteen…[she's thinking]…15 or 16 one of 'em. But I know I got bored in school. Then I went to drinking and smoking weed. I said okay. I got to taste of that doggone free life and that was it.

David: You say you got a taste of the free life?

Angela: Yeah.

Then she volunteers the next phases of her girlhood, detailing her free life.

Angela: I start going out. Daddy wanna give me a curfew. I said okay.

[He said] You got to be in the house around bout 10' o'clock [10pm]

If not you not gonna get in the house. I said okay… [she says sarcastically]

So…[pause] I did it for a while.

David: So, at age 15 …16…you were born 1961. It had to be around 1976/ 1977 when you dropped out school…a few years after your brother was murdered?

Angela: Yeah.

I'm also in this moment calculating out loud a timeline based on my mother's birth. In doing so, a lot of her actions pivot around/ shortly after her brother's death. I wonder now what their relationship was like? Did his death shock her? How did his death impact her and her decisions about life and school? This is the non-emotional void that seems to exist at this time of her life.

"And so you had a taste of the free life," I say to her, calculating my next question. I wanted to ask if her turning to these social vices was in response to her brother's death, but for some reason, I didn't. Instead, I ask an equally vital question about her sex life.

David: Now with you tasting this new free life… were you a virgin at the time? Because you said you started going out? If you were not a virgin? When did you start to visit your sex life as a young person?

My mother then quips back with:

Angela: Think back. I had Darrel when I was 14.

David: Oh, that's seventh grade or so. So you had always… [been that]

My mother laughed.

We both laugh.

David: Now as a young person I have to ask you this. Were you sexually abused growing up? And if so, did that have any influence on how you experienced your sexuality?

Angela: No. No No No. I was not sexually abused. I wasn't that.

David: Your sex life started at a young age?

Angela: I just had a high sex drive.

David: High sex drive. [I repeat before laughing]. Then we laugh together.

Angela: Is that a problem?

With that question posed back to me, I think the question of her sexuality followed my mother throughout her life. A young Black girl having babies had to be just about a 'ho… whore. My mother's quip, and as evidenced in our discourse here, suggests that she was sexually actualized and fully aware of her sexuality. She had no shame and embraced this aspect of her Black girl self—against discourses that shamed Black girls and women who freely and openly expressed their sexuality when they should have been, as my mother often was, at church.

In listening to my mother speak about her childhood, and especially the death of her mother and grandmother, I can't help but think about how this loss shaped her own consciousness as a mother. Had her life turned out differently had her mother and grandmother lived long enough to love her into adulthood?

My mother, on her own volition, and on account of her own actions, experienced adultification without much guidance. She was a young parent who tasted the free life and, I sense, hungered for that freedom for years—wanting to taste that initial taste, chasing, always running toward it. And she did it at a great cost.

Trauma, grief, and a bit of sexual agency shaped my mother's becoming, and while the degree to which these impacted her life is immeasurable, their weight crushed all in her path.

4
Angela

My mother is dark skinned and as a girl growing up in Jacksonville, Florida, a defining feature was her long, long, black hair. My mother's long hair attracted everyone—girls who thought her hair fake and… men. I remember often watching my mother style her hair. She would curl her hair, straighten her hair, brush her hair, pin her hair up in a bun or simply wear it lose down her back. Her hair was beautiful. When she started doing drugs, her hair grew ugly. I first noticed the change in my mother's hair when I visited her in jail. There she sat, behind an enclosed glass shield, talking to us on the phone, wearing that iconic orange jump suit and her once long hair, now a short frizzy afro.

You see, when my mother left for Pic-N-Save on that early day in August 1994, she was not gone for three years, as I imagined she was. Before returning home after the third year, my mother spent time in jail. She was arrested, convicted, and sentenced to the local jail for both stealing a check from a woman's check book and fraudulently using that check in an attempt to pay rent.

By that time, my mother was separated from my father and involved with a man named Frank. I didn't know much about Frank but what I do know is that he beat my mother, used drugs with my mother, and lived with us for years before he moved to Georgia, where my mother soon followed him. When my mother went to jail, I would go to live with Frank's people on the East-Side of town—because, little did I know, my grandfather Eddie was dying and could no longer look after me.[9] Frank's family took me to see my mother in jail. With them, I started fourth grade at Andrew A. Robinson Elementary school, located a few blocks down from the Pic-N-Save where my mother claimed she went to school shop for me to purchase the Sonic the Hedge Hog Trapper Keeper.

This chapter accounts for my mother's drug use and domestic violence. I ask my mother why she left us for Frank, what was her relationship with him, and how she met him. She breathes deeply throughout, taking pauses to grapple with the weight of this conversation—which, we both know was coming.

David: **Because you say you started smoking weed in the 1970s and drinking.... How soon after that did you meet Frank?**

Angela: Okay...let me see ...that was [pause]... That was before you were born?

David: **So, several years. That's almost ten years?**

Angela: Yes. I met him in '84.

David: **You met him when I was born?**

Angela: I met him before you were born. Because when you were born I don't know where your daddy was at. Because when he left the house that Friday...I say, David, I'm goin' in labor. Because I used to stay up at night looking at Preacher Creature. Late Friday night. And I was going into labor with you. I told him before he left the house...David, I'm going into labor.

"oh, I'll be back before you go into labor"

I ain't see him until that Sat'day morning. Where the hell you come from?

David: After you had me?

Angela: Hmmmhmm

David: So that was uhhh…[I'm silent]…

My mother continues to vent about my Daddy not being present at the hospital during my birth.

Angela: Where was you at?

My mother mentions quickly that my dad began to ask about me. But she interrupts that memory and continues to vent:

Angela: …when I told you I was going into labor you left the house[.] I had to call the ambulance.

As my mother continues to speak, I notice her language construction, where she seems to leave the interview and begin to speak not just about my father but, it seems, directly to him. Confronting him for not being at the hospital at the time of my birth.

After allowing this moment to pass, I shift the conversation back to Frank.

David: Now, I'm gonna go back to Frank. You met Frank sometime after I was born or little before I was born?

Angela: Yeah

David: So, between 1980 and 1984…

Angela: In '84.

David: **Now, how did you meet him?**

Angela: [silence. Thinking]. I was going to the clinic. I always went the back way when I was pregnant with you.

David: **You were walking to the clinic pregnant with me?**

Angela: Yeah. I always went the back [way]…[the] short cut to get there. And look like he just stood out to me.

[silence]

He said, "hey," and I said hey and we went to talkin.' But I said I'll talk to you [later] because I got to go to the clinic.

David: **How did he stand out to you?**

Angela: I reckon it was his height.

David: **Hmmm. I remember him being tall. And you being very short. After you said I'll speak to you later and you had me, how soon after that you two began to date?**

Angela: After you was born? I think a year or two years. [pause] Yeah Because after that, David went..[pause]. I didn't know nothin 'bout

Shirley.

Again, my mother shifts the conversation away from Frank back toward my father, David Sr, and his infidelity. This time, I listened to the conversation intently. She discusses my father having an affair with Shirley, my younger brother Eric's mother. I'm learning that my mother's memories of her relationships with men are entangled between herself, my father, and Frank.

Angela: I didn't really know nothing about Shirley. That's when I found out she was pregnant

David: **With Eric?**

Angela: Yes. So, I say [to David Sr], you been stepping on me all dis long time? So you trynna' tell me that you were messing… stepping out…when I went into labor?

David: **"Oh Jesus," I say**.

My mom goes silent for a bit.

David: **So, daddy was cheating?**

Angela: Yes [she says affirmatively]. A longtime.

My mother continues uninterrupted.

Angela: I've always been the type to stay home. And stay in the house while he was out here doing what he wanted to do.

After a brief pause, I enter back into the conversation:

David. **So, you met Frank and you decided at that time that you wanted to be with Frank for what reasons?**

Angela: [Silent a bit] What other reasons that I have beside your daddy going [and] getting another woman pregnant?

David: **I have no idea momma, I'm not chu [slang for you].**

She laughs a bit.

Angela: He went […she then jumbles her words a bit].

Though hardly perceptible from her jumbled rambling, I hear that one reason that my mother decided to "go with" Frank was that my daddy got Shirley pregnant. My dad was cheating on my mom at the very moment that she was pregnant with me. She repeats this memory often in this moment.

After making sense of my mother's otherwise jumbled reflection, I then pose the question of revenge.

David: **So, you got with Frank to get back at daddy?**

Angela: No. I just wanted to get the hell away from him [my daddy].

David: **So, you didn't really like Frank? You just saw this as an opportunity to get away from your husband?**

Angela: Thank you [she says, agreeing with my reading of her starting to date Frank].

I then break into laughter and told my mom that she should have talked to me about this. Of course, I'm joking around because what would I, at the age of toddler, know about the messy drama of dating?

I continue to ask about Frank.

David: **So, now you're with Frank. In 1984…[wait] a year after I was born. And you stay with him for quite some time? Because I remember Liberty Street.**

Angela: Yeah. That was liberty street.

Liberty Street is my earliest memory of the house we lived in as a "family"—my mother, two sisters, and two brothers, with Frank. Although the house is now marked as a historic site in the Springfield Neighborhood of Jacksonville, Florida, it was first an old, not quite run down, large house. It had a large wrap-around porch that connected the front and side doors. I'd run along this porch and through the house playing chase with my siblings and even my mother. We had a few dogs; there was an old typewriter on the side porch that I'd "play-play" type on, and a raggedy fence enclosed the perimeter of the house.

Figure 8 The House on Liberty Street. The first home I lived in with my mother and siblings. The home has been renovated with new fencing. Picture taken December 28, 2024.

I begin attending daycare when we lived in that house off Liberty Street. And I remember the first day when my mother dropped me off to daycare. I was mad, crying hysterically, and just as she put me down, I slapped her in the face.

During our conversation about us living on Liberty Street, and the memories of me starting daycare, my mother told me that she was forced to put me in daycare so that she could continue to receive Food Stamps. Furthermore, the social worker told my mother that if she wished to receive food stamps, then she'd have to attend WIC[10] Classes. Although frustrated by this new rule and by the invasive social worker, my mother obliged and off to daycare I went…in the name of providing food for the family.

After Liberty Street, we all moved to Palm Terrace. Then back on the Eastside to a duplex unit that eventually burned down. My mother injured her wrist as she rescued us all from our downstairs apartment—for it was the upstairs unit that was on fire, which, furthermore, was started by a woman who threw her cigarette on the bed during a heated argument with her boyfriend. Her infant baby died in the fire.

There is a scar on my mother's wrist that archives this moment. Suddenly homeless, we stayed in a hotel, La Quinta, where my mom worked, for a short bit of time. After La Quinta, we moved into a cute little house on West 22nd Street and Pearl Street— down the street from Brentwood Apartments, where my aunt Deborah lived for the rest of her life. I attended Brentwood Elementary for third grade.

As we moved, Frank was always there, moving right along with us. So, I asked my mother, again, why she decided to be with Frank before I realized she'd answered this question.

My mother continues to state her reason: because of my father's infidelity. But this time, she mentions their violent relationship and her nearly killing him in defense of her own life.

Angela: That man [almost] made me kill him.

My interest in Frank and him beating my mother compelled my mother further to speak about my father.

David: **So, you experienced abusive relationships in your life from men?**

Angela: Yes…

As she responds to this question, her voice trails off a bit. For me, her diminished voice signals her hesitancy to admit that truth.

David: **From your husband, my daddy, and was that a driving force for why you wanted to leave him as well?**

Angela: Yeah, I likely killed him.

David: **You almost killed him?**

Angela: If it weren't be for my cousin Hollis that stayed with us right there on 3rd and Walnut. He stopped me from killin'em.

David: **When you say you were about to kill'em what were you about to kill'em with?**

Angela: A knife.

I speak ineffably. Shocked, I think. My mother continues…

Angela: If it don't be for my cousin when he walked in that kitchen. Where David cornered me at. When I picked up that knife I was going straight for his heart.

Her cousin Hollis walked right into the kitchen and grabbed the knife out of her hand.

David: **Momma, why did he corner you?**

Angela: I done forgot what me and him was ah'gin [arguing] bout. I was in the kitchen finna start cooking.

Silence.

I was finna start cooking. Frying some chicken. And I don't know where he come from but he cornered me. When he hit me. He cornered me in that kitchen. If it don't be for my cousin Hollis that knife was going straight to his heart.

David: **He hit you? [Before I can fully ask the question my mom answers quickly]**

Angela: Yes.

David: **He just came in the house and hit you?**

Angela: I don't know where he come from but I was in the kitchen. I was frying some chicken. That's what I was doin' because I had left off da porch.

David: **And he hit you in the face? Or in the back…or…?**

Angela: He hit me in my face. When he did. When he spun me around. I spun around and picked up that knife. I don't know where my cousin come from but he came in dat kitchen because I was finna stab him straight in the damn heart with it.

David: **And so, by that time you'd had had enough of the abuse? (She answers before I continue my question).**

Angela: Yes.

David: **Because he was very abusive throughout the relationship?**

Angela: I got tired of dat.

My mother then continues without me asking any questions.

Angela: I know one time I was pregnant wit'chu and I was on the sofa.

Silence.

> And I had just got through drinkin' a damn pepsi-cola in the 16oz bottle and he mess around here and pull my leg off dat sofa and I took dat 16 oz bottle…and if he wouldn't have ducked I'd hit him dead in the head wit'it.

David: **He pulled you in a violent way?**

Angela: Yes. Off the damn sofa.

David: **And you were pregnant with me? How many months were you pregnant?**

Angela: I was…8 months pregnant.

David: **Oh Jesus. I could'a died.**

My mother then repeats that she nearly hit my daddy in the head with the Pepsi bottle. I nearly say something—"and he pulled you"—but can't quite complete my thoughts. I'm shocked speechless.

My mother continues:

Angela: I done told you…My daddy didn't put his hands on me. So, what the hell…make you think I'mma let'chu do it?

David: **He pulled you from the leg. Did you fall off the couch?**

Angela: Yeah, I feel off the couch. That's when I picked that damn bottle up

David: **And…but I wasn't injured? Your pregnancy wasn't injured?**

Angela: No.

David: **Okay.**

Repetition: My mother repeats the details of this story with clarity. When I tried to move the story forward, she dwelled there, in the near killing of my dad and the violence.

Repetition here speaks to the trauma that continues to live within my mother's body. While she does not remember her mother telling her that she loved her, as I discuss in the previous chapter—or as she says, "I can't remember all that"—she remembers with great detail the violence of her life. The imprint of violence on my mother's psyche is deep and permanent.

I then circle back to Frank and repeat the questions that I asked before.

David: **So, Frank comes along –when did the abuse start and did you ever feel like you wanted to leave?**

Angela: Hmmm [takes a breath]. Lemme see. Where were staying over there off of Liberty street.

David: **Liberty, you say momma?**

Angela: Hmmhmm.

          I really don't know what the hell was wrong with dat… [trails off]

For one thang, he thought I wanted his damn brother. What the fuck do I want with your brother?

What I want with hiiiiimmmmm? [my mother asks dramatically]

Figure 9 Liberty & 9th, The house on Liberty sat at the intersection of these streets. Picture taken December 28, 2024.

David: **So, he [Frank] thought you wanted [his brother Randy] so he just began beating you, for whatever reason, including that one?**

Angela: Yeah [my mother shouts. And is getting very vocal]

What the hell do I want with your damn brother?

Like before, when speaking about my daddy, my mother's language construction displaces me and allows her to speak directly to Frank—as if he's here in the interview.

David: Hmmhmm. And then we move to Palm Terrace.

Before I ask a direct question, I step away from being an interviewer and just show up as my mother's son. And share with my mother how I too have lived with the terror of domestic violence.

One day, my mother picked me up from school, Mary McLeod Bethune—I was in either Kindergarten or first grade. After picking up the paper food stamps from the Welfare Office off Golfair Boulevard, we went grocery shopping. We then went home to put up the groceries but didn't have a chance to because Frank ambushed my mother.

David: And I remember one day, he [Frank] came up and he clothe-lined you and dragged you from the living room way back to your bedroom and began beating you. And I was just standing at the door. And I just froze. And I was like what is...

My voice suddenly trails off...

And so, I remember the beating taking place that day and I kept thinking to myself (as an adult years later): I wonder how many times when we kids were not home, and at school for instance, that you suffered the violence of this man. Because I don't know what your life was like when were at school.

So, did he beat you when no one was home?

Angela: [long pause] No. Because daddy [Eddie] would come there.

I then share inner thoughts with my mom that I'd never said to her before.

David: I just remember I kept thinking to myself: My mom doesn't deserve this. She is a really sweet woman. Who is this man? And I kept always thinking to myself, why is she with him?

My mother is silent. Listening. I'm not asking questions. Just releasing.

I wanted my mother to know and hear my inner thoughts and the trauma-memories that lived with her boychild. Lives with me still.

I then return to asking questions about her choice to stay with Frank:

David: So, what was it about him that made you want to just stay with him? After all those terrible moments with him. The violence. And the abuse?

Angela: I don't know.

David: You don't know?

Angela: I think I blocked that shit out my mind. I think I really did.

David: You blocked what out your mind?

Angela: Him.

David: So, when you left him you blocked it all out?

Angela: Yeah (she states vocally).

She stammers a few words and then says:

"I was thinking…wait a minute. Hold on. What was I thinking about?"

My mother left Frank many, many years later. We lived in Palm Terrace in the early 1990s. She finally returned home to Jacksonville, for good, shortly before I graduated high school in 2003. She'd visit Jacksonville here and there but would return to be with Frank in Georgia just as often in the intervening years.

We then enter a conversation about the times she left and returned to Jacksonville. I shared with her that Hattie and I have different memories of these moments. In my memory, and I share this with my mother, she returned home, briefly, in 1997, during the time my sister Devita was pregnant with her now only child: she, like my mother, was 14.

Whatever the memory, there was always the pull of Frank.

David: Now, I've asked you this before momma, but replay it again. Did he [Frank] introduce you to the drugs? The crack?

Angela: Yes.

She states this again with a somber, nearly, regretful tone. Not as sharp when compared to answering in the affirmative about violence, for example.

David: And how old were you?

Angela: Ooh.   Let's   see…[silence]…Early   twenties.   Mid-twenties…?

David: You were in your early twenties. I know that because we were in Palm Terrace. And your hair was very long. And before going to work you would spend a lot of time doing your hair. Curling your hair with those ugly pink curlers [to which she laughs].

So, he introduced you to drugs. And you were on drugs for…do you know how many years you were on drugs?

Angela: It was way long. I can't even count the number of years.

David: Would you say five years, ten years?

Angela: [long silence]

I would say…[in coherent chatter. Then very clearly]

I stopped using drugs the day I turned 50.

Remember my mother was born on February 24, 1961.

I then proceed to calculate the years with her out loud, from her early twenties. Then I say.

David: So, that's like thirty years momma.

Angela: Hmmhmm [she agrees].

David: That's three decades.

After a considerable pause, I proceed.

David: When you left us, me…and you decided to go move with Frank…you decided to leave. Do you know why? Or can you recall why you decided to spend most of your time with Frank?

Angela: [very very long pause]

I went to stay with Frank. I was with your Daddy…

I hear my mother start to cry.

David: **Momma are you okay?**

Angela: Yeah.

[silence]

I wasn't intended to stay that long.

[silence]

But for some reason I did. I wasn't intended to stay that long.

[then incoherent utters]

When I first got there I got me a job. But that job didn't work out because me and the doggone owner didn't get along

David: **You stayed there because you started to find a life while you were working?**

Angela: [long silence] Yeah.

David: **Did you have any kind of relationship with Frank in Georgia? What was the relationship like when you left for those years?**

Angela: [silence]

No.

Because he really didn't have a place to stay on his damn own.

When I got there to Georgia. He stayed on the farm in a trailer with some dude. But he was working on the farm. So, [silence]…he would go to town to get groceries. Come back. I was out there on da farm. I didn't mind it because [coughs] I didn't have nothing to do.

So then, in the summer time. The man hired me caused they wanted me to [work] with squash.

I wasn't finna get down there and pick no gawtdamn squash.

David: **When you were there were you in a relationship with Frank? Were you his girlfriend? How would you describe that?**

Angela: He was somebody I was with.

David: **And did you love him?**

Angela: And did how spell that word? [here is my mother's classic sass and whit]

David: **[laughing] I spell it aloud. L.O.V.E.**

Angela: Well, I don't know how to spell it when I was with him.

I laugh!

Angela: I couldn't do that one.

My mother didn't love Frank at all. I revisit the question of why she left us for him, once more.

David: **Why do you leave us, momma?**

Angela: [long silence.]

I was following my head.

David.   **And what was in your head at the time?**

Angela: What was in my head at that time...? I was on those doggone drugs.

1. Her legacy

I won my first essay competition in fifth grade, when, having left after second grade, I returned to Bethune Elementary. I wrote an essay for the D.A.R.E. Program, and specifically their Just Say No! Program. Before I knew about metaphors or symbols as literary devices, I used them to talk about drug addiction. You see, in that essay, I wrote about a fish, worm, and a hook. What I remember most about that essay is that I wrote that the worm works as a ruse that fools the fish into believing that he's there to fulfill the fish's hunger, when quite the contrary, the worm-as-ruse is designed to kill the fish.

In truth, I was writing about my mother's own drug addiction. She, in my fifth-grade mind, was the fish whose hunger for crack nearly killed her. I also remember the thunderous applause and standing ovation that I received after reading my essay. Although the essay won first place, I'm not sure if the essay was really that good. Though, the degree to which I personalized the harm of drug diction and that I gave it a face—my mother's Black woman face—played into the fictions of Black motherhood that under-wrote much of the DARE program's ideologies and its Moynihan-influenced policies.[11] In short, as I wrote of my mother as the fish hungering for the worm, it confirmed for DARE officials that Black mothers, especially those on welfare, are harmful to their kids and communities. "My mother is the fish. She is addicted to drugs. She got hooked. I no longer live with her. She left me. The drugs took my mother."

I would go on to write numerous college admissions essays, scholarship essays, and fellowship essays echoing this narrative sentiment—my mother left me. Drugs. My mother left me. On repeat. Indeed, in these essays my mother's story of her drug use and abandoning her kids looms largely. Throughout these writings, my mother was a rhetorical device, a literary conceit, that held together and motivated my thoughts simultaneously. In these stories, I spoke from my personal experiences and sec-ondhand accountings of my mother's absence.

The historian in me now understands that my mother didn't just happen to find drugs. The Regan Administration facilitated the mass infiltration of crack cocaine into poor and inner-city neigh-borhoods as a part of its effort to crack down on crime and "the war on drugs." In the wake of Ronald Regan's political machine, his wife Nancy Regan helped launch the DARE Program and its slo-gan "Just Say No." While I cannot quite say that my mother would have lived a drug-free life if it were not for Frank, it doesn't escape me that her, and the lives of poor Black people, were entrenched by anti-Black policies designed to ensnare the whole of the inner-city. My mother was in part, a pawn (and not a worm) in a larger political game.

In speaking with my mother, I no longer speak from secondhand experiences but with the might of learned history and my moth-er's voice. Whether or not folx are swayed by her story matters less than her having a chance to speak her own truth.

My mother is not perfect and she made some life changing, con-sequential decisions. Yes, I spent years angry at her. Being cold toward her when she returned. But I was hurting, too. My mother had returned home but not to the same innocent June Bug that she left many years prior. I was mad as hell because the person I loved the most had left and came back like nothing happened.

In my mother's absence though, I have inherited the most invaluable thing we can have in this life: love. And this love came from my sisters. This love came from people around me who did their best to love me. This love came from hoping to share this love with my mother should she return.

She did. And I was unable. Until now. Well, a few years back, but you get my point.

In closing, I asked my mother this final question:

David: So far in this life, what do you feel is the best thing you've done?

Angela: The best thing I have done. I came back home to my kids.

David: Why is that the best thing?

Angela: [Silence].

She attempted to say something but didn't.

I let her know that her kids love her. Then I say:

David: I'm writing this book for you and for our family and no one else.

Angela: Lemme say one thing baby. I am so proud of you and I love you so much.

David: I love you, too, Momma.

End Note: My mother died in the early morning hours of January 8, 2025. She died from colon-rectal cancer in the hospice unit of the very hospital that her mother died: St. Vincent. In the months prior

Figure 10 My mother and me having dinner at Buffalo Wild Wings in Jacksonville, FL, 2021.

to this interview, my mother urged me to come home to Jakconville for the holidays, so that she could, from the bottom of her heart, say goodbye.

Part III
School

Figure 11 Douglas Anderson School of the Arts. Jacksonville, FL. Picture taken December 28, 2024.

5
Sissy/ Flute

Is that a flute? Boy, what are you doing with a flute?

—My Auntie

―――

On one balmy afternoon, sometime in 1997, my aunt Kay Kay—who lived on Leonard Circle in a ranch-style home that she inherited from her mother and was located in the area that we didn't know was called Brown's Dump—stepped out on the front porch. For what? I don't know. I was busily practicing my flute—just a toot-tooting when the sounds of my aunt's sharply sweet voice cut through the summer's air, halting my tooting.

"Is that a flute?"

And before I could say anything, she continued:

"Boy, what are you doing with a flute?"

My aunt Kay Kay is a lovely woman, who, shortly after my grandfather died in 1995—and after my mother first left for Georgia—took my sisters and me to live with her. We were living with my father for the first time, and then suddenly we weren't.

Anyhow, my auntie had, for the most part, served as a mother-like figure for my eldest sister, Ann. Additionally, aunt Kay Kay herself had two young boys that she was raising as a single mother. How she managed to provide all that she did for my sisters, me, and her two boys, I don't know. To this day, she works in the medical field continuing the same career she had when we went to live with her. Like my own mother, aunt Kay Kay had long beautiful hair that she styled with a French-role—the look back in the day (google it!)!

Each day before work, she turned her radio clock to the latest gospel hit and adorned herself with her crisp, very white, work uniform. As she dressed for work, she brewed coffee that perfumed the house with the smell of burnt walnut and sugar. Everything about her was just so sweet.

In fact, living with her, at least for me, felt like the good life. There was cable television and she served breakfast, lunch, and dinner, daily; the backyard was fully equipped with a complete swing-set: sliding board and all; she owned a washer and dryer that was located in its own laundry room, so there was no need to go to the laundromat and spend, god knows, how much money; she drove a sporty white Honda Coup before purchasing a stylish white Acura with black leather seats; there was video game consoles with endless games. Yes honey, her home was fully loaded with what we needed to simply enjoy ourselves. And even though there were times in school where my fifth-grade teacher, Mr Hill, had to call her with news of my bad behavior, and while she was a caring disciplinarian, I always felt her care for my sisters and me deep within my bones. And to this day, I still do.

That's why, in the context of my auntie's typical sweetness and otherwise luxurious life, her question stung me. For a moment I froze, suspended mid-air by her curiosity and… *judgement.*

"Yes," I say with a shaking timid voice. "It's a flute."

She stared a bit and only in the way that southern Black women stare: squinted her eyes, slightly tilted head. After a few more seconds of staring in *southern Black woman judgment*, she fixed her position, painted her face with a charming smile, and headed back into the house. To do what, I don't know. I resumed my toot-tooting.

I knew what my auntie was thinking—flutes were for girls. Many, everyone really, said flutes were for girls. Meaning only girls play the flute. And the clarinet. Boys play the trumpet, the tuba, the saxophone, and, oh yes, the DRUMS.

If you looked at the flute section in the bands at my middle school—it seemed true: all the flute players, and most of the clarinet players, were girls. Atleast at both Eugene Butler Middle School and Twin Lakes Academy Middle..

Oh, I also played the clarinet. In fact, as I discuss later, my first instrument was the bass clarinet--pronounced "base clarinet"--before switching to the B-flat clarinet, the one mostly girls play. I switched to the flute a year after playing the clarinet.

In either case, I was a flute-a-tootin' Black sissy.

Yet, in the face of these stereotypes, my entry into music resulted in something equally more powerful. Love. In and through music, I found love. Love for music, yes, but also the type of love often buried beneath narratives of life in the inner-city. Black gay love.

This chapter is about love and rage.

1. Eugene Butler Middle School

"Off the list in '96. Off the list in '96." Students, faculty, and staff, all shout-sang this mantra throughout the halls, when, after years of receiving failing test scores by the district and state, Eugene Butler Middle school was no longer graded an "F" school. As a result of improved state-wide test scores across all grade-levels, Butler, as the school was known, received in 1996, a passing grade by the state. After Principal Murry shared this news over the PA system, the school celebrated thunderously and every student received a gift: a white shirt decorated with the school's colors—red and black—and the infamous "off the list" slogan emblazoned across the top of the shirt. We received our shirts on the school's field, where loud music blasted from stereos and everyone wasn't just at the gym but attending a school-sponsored bar-b-que.

Although still located at 900 Acorn Street, the middle school has a new name: "Young Men's and Women's Leadership Academy." I still gag at the name change and the district's attempt to erase the school's name from history. Even more, student learning is now segregated by gender—"boys" on one floor, with "girls" on the other. I'll reserve my judgment at the school's new direction by stating that despite the name change, as of year 2024, the school's buildings all look just the same as they did in 1996.

In 1996, and for years before, Butler, like many inner-city schools throughout Jacksonville, was a poorly resourced school. Mostly Black students attended the school—though a very small number of white students were bussed to Butler and were all in advanced classes. For the most part, most of the teachers were white. Yeah, we had Black teachers, but in very small numbers—my geography teacher, Mr White, was Black! Mr Murry, the school's principal was Black. Mrs Jennings, a Language Arts teacher was Black. All the male coaches were Black, and one of the Dean of Students was Black: the incomparable Ms Chapman. She was MEAN, too! Though, I'd eventually come to like her. The School's Resource Officer, a *very* handsome, tall, and actually gun-toting cop, was Black.

I'm sure there were a few more, but I don't remember their names.

Anyhow, Butler was a lively school. Lively because there was always music vibrating from the walls of the school's halls. Students created this music by beat-boxing; they also rhythmically used their knuckles on walls to create beats; they shout, call-and-response style, either their respective grade levels or which side of town or whatever neighborhood they lived in. Eastside was often followed by a louder, Westside!

There was, of course, a lot of fighting. Every day, it seemed. Sometimes, there would be a buildup to a fight. Sometimes, fights broke out simultaneously—at lunch, or between "class periods," in the hallways.

What I don't ever recall was gun violence—though, many folx made these gross, unfair, and wrong assumptions about our school.

I personally, at Butler, was bullied a lot.

When pushed, or when I simply got tired of being afraid, or turning the cold cheek, I fought back.

I also didn't take much crap from the teachers. Especially not the white teachers.

2. *"Get out of my classroom, you little punk"*

My sixth grade Language Arts teacher told the school Principal, Mr Murry, that I threatened her life. She, of course, lied. No lie, I had a lot of behavioral problems in school. If I felt that a teacher disrespected me, oh honey, I'd disrespect them right back—and I mean curse their asses out. The teacher's name was Mrs Thomas, and she and I got into it that day—maybe I was talking during a lesson or a test. Whatever the case, I'm sure I was doing something that she didn't want me to do. After going back and forth with her, she finally threw me out of the class and locked the door. I beat on the door. Even kicked it. Because I was mad as hell. But, I'm certain, I never threatened her.

As a result, I was nearly expelled from the school district—every school in Duval County. Mr Murry, who again was also a Black man, believed my teacher—who was a white woman. During that meeting, he didn't hold back on how angry the situation made him—though, he was clearly performing for Mrs Thomas. White feminine fragility holds such power over some Black men. For whatever reason, thank God, he only suspended me for a week.

Because my suspension was immediate, I left Mr Murry's Office and walked home. My thoughts were empty, yet I was expecting my mother to be home. She wasn't. She was home before I'd left for school that morning. My dad always went to work by 5 am and came home by 5 pm. When I got home that day of my first time being suspended at Butler, nobody was home.

That night, my mother didn't return. My father had. My dad hardly knew what was going on with me at school—he just worked, paid the bills, bought the food, and sometimes cooked. His peace was him sitting on the front porch in his tattered, ugly green, recliner chewing tobacco after work—mostly shirtless, sockless, and shoeless. He also enjoyed the weekend and spent his Fridays drinking out at whatever bar men of his country ilk attended. He slept in on Saturdays and Sundays—the days he didn't work.

That whole week, though, my mother did not return home. Some of us were concerned, is she in jail again?

Nevertheless, during that week, I moseyed about the house. Doing nothing. After my suspension ended, I returned to school with the intent of being on my best behavior. That hope lasted only a few days. In math class, the boys picked on me a lot.

Faggot. Sissy. Dirty as punk.

I enjoyed learning math, so I did my best to pay those lil boys no mind.

However, Mr Jones, my math teacher, hardly stopped them. So, one day, when I decided to defend myself against their taunting, turning to face them—they sat behind me—Mr Jones jumped down my throat. He began yelling at me and insisted that I should have continued to give them the cold shoulder.

Again, feeling disrespected, I went off on him and, like Mrs Thomas, he, threw me out of the classroom.

"Who are you talking to like that? You ain't said shit to them all period and now you wanna stop because I said something back to them?"

They had been "messing" with me for the entire class period so I said to Mr Jones something about him fearing them—being afraid of them, and him needing to grow some balls. Of course, my words triggered him and challenged his own, yet otherwise fragile white masculinity.

"Get outta my class…you little punk."

And boom, without much thought, I left him and those repressed gay boys to their own devices, eating each other, I'm sure!

Unlike Mrs Thomas, Mr Jones didn't write me up on a referral, which would have sent me to the Dean's Office, and to the very strict, mean, Ms Chapman. So, I just lolly-gagged out in the hall way. I decided not to knock or kick on the door because I knew where that would lead—back to Mr Murry's Office and expulsion for sure.

After a few minutes, Mr Jones came out of the class and tried to reason with me. And because I was fed up with him, I ignored the hell out of him. My passive aggressiveness must have enraged him further because he started cursing like a sailor. At this moment, I looked at him, shocked that this white man was goin' in on me like this—me, one of few students who actually paid attention to his whack ass math lessons, givin' him a chance to teach us po' inner city kids—and just stormed off. Where to, I wasn't exactly sure—I just knew I needed to get away from Mr Jones!

"Where are you going? Get back here you little punk…"

"Fuck you" and often I went.

3. Ms Milby

I must have walked only a few feet before being stopped in my tracks by the most beautiful sound I'd ever heard coming from the school's bandroom.

She was playing an instrument I'd never heard of.

She sounded soooo good.

I walked closer to the door to peek inside the classroom. There she stood. Unaware of me. Poised, elegant, and spinning silk from her flute.

Her name was Natoya, and she was one of the most popular girls in school. I knew her, and I knew that she was in the band but I didn't know she sounded like that! Everyday, we walked home from school together. She bought me cookies with the money she always had, and she was one of my first friends I made that year in sixth grade—her and Charlotte.

Anyhow, in those moments at the door, I just listened to her until the bell rang—signaling the end of one class period and the beginning of the next. Students began to file into the hallways and, to my delight, into the bandroom. The clanging of chairs and dropping of bags harmonized with the click-clacking of cases, small and large, as everyone began to take out instruments of all kinds. Trumpets, clarinets, saxophones, tubas. And then, within minutes, a short, stout, white woman, with curly blond short hair, and a collared shirt tucked into her khaki pants, entered the room wearing tennis shoes and had what I thought was a stick in her hand. Just before she started to speak, I suddenly remembered that I needed to get to my next class, Science with Mrs Westbury. My favorite class!

That day, I went home thinking about band—I wondered how to get into band.

I wrote a letter to the teacher, expressing my interest in joining band. I would soon find out the band teacher's name: Ms Milby. All that was left to do was figure out how to give her the letter. My scheming and sleuthing took some time. I observed when the band room was empty and slipped in during those zone-free times. I located Ms Milby's office and slipped my letter under her door. My heart was racing!

Nothing at first.

A whole nine weeks had passed before any action followed.

Then one day, while I was in the hallway walking to, from, or probably even being kicked out of another class, she called for me.

"Are you David Green?"

"Yes?"

"Come with me."

Without hesitation, yet with a racing heart, I followed her to the bandroom and we sat in her cramped office.

"I received your letter a few weeks ago. I see that you want to be in the band?"

I nodded my head.

"Why? What sparks your interest in music?"

I was silent. And shrugged my shoulders.

I was nervous as hell. And I couldn't tell her that hearing Natoya play her flute sparked my interest.

"What instrument do you want to play?"

I didn't see a flute, but I did see a music book with an instrument gracing its cover.

"That one," I pointed to the picture of the clarinet.

Ms Milby turned to look at the picture. She smiled as she turned back toward me.

"We'd have to change your schedule immediately. Are you okay with that?"

I shake my head yes and smile, big, half crying. I'd have to drop my computer class with Mr McInnish to make room for my newly chosen elective.

"Welcome to Band" she said, and she hugs me.

The process of changing my schedule was simple and the next day, I had "Beginner's Band" on my schedule for the second nine-weeks—and the rest of the school year.

As I walked into Band class though, Ms Milby greeted me with less than good news.

"We don't have any more clarinets. But we do have a similar instrument. Here, this one. It's called the bass clarinet. We can start you on this instrument and when we find a B-flat clarinet you can move to that section."

I look over at the clarinet section...all Black girls, judging me with their piercing eyes.

Although unfortunate, I said, "Okay."

I didn't play the first few days. Ms Milby just asked me to watch. She gave me music books to study. To learn music notes, staffs, time signatures, and the fingerings of the bass clarinet and B-flat clarinet.

Each day after school I studied those books with an intense focus. For hours on the back porch of my father's house—on McConihe Street—I would practice the fingerings of both the B-flat and bass clarinet. Because I physically had one, I'd practice blowing into the bass clarinet. I learned to soak the thick reed with timely precision. I'd learn the notes to that semester's band music while putting to memory all that my brain had the capacity to store. I was hooked and soon became the 1st Chair bass clarinet player in Eugene Butler's Beginner's Band.

4. The clarinet thief

My focus on the music helped me absorb the reality that my mother was gone. I cried and poured myself into the music. In the sounds of *Chorale and Allegro*, theme songs to films such as *Chariots of Fire* and Disney classics such as *The Lion King*, *The Little Mermaid* and *Pocahontas*, and even fine-tuning the school's Fight Song, I escaped into another place, a third dimension of sound; and I did so until graduating from high school. Music became a muse, to which I gave my heart.

Yet, the story of me discovering band does not end here.

I still wanted to play the B-flat clarinet, but I didn't own one. I realized that the clarinet was a popular instrument—which meant that one would never become available to me. So, I stole one from a local high school and without questioning how my family could afford to purchase me an instrument, Ms Milby moved me from bass clarinet to B-flat clarinet, and much to the chagrin of the girls who were, seemingly, far advanced than me. But they were in fact threatened by my presence because, and I say this with utter truth, I was REALLY good. I had nothing else to do but practice, and I did so for hours. I learned every band selection by memory—every song, from concert band to marching band. Oh, the girls hated me and called me every name in the book, all of which by this time, I'd heard and gotten used to. "Why don't you play the trumpet? Clarinet is for girls."

I played on and when, in seventh grade, the bullying by one of the "clarinet girls" became so bad, I told my sister Devita. She met the girl in the cafeteria one day and whipped her ass. Ms Chapman suspended both of us for a few days. I played my clarinet all throughout my suspension. I returned to school, to band, and to no more of that girl's bullying.

After joining the band, I hardly got into any more trouble at school. In seventh grade, I was only suspended once—after kicking these twins' asses. One twin, who was taunting me in science class, only waited until gym class to confront me. He and his twin brother had gym class together. Initially, I feared getting jumped, so I avoided gym class for a few days. Then, on about the fourth day, I was sick of being afraid and decided to go to gym class. I was fully aware that he and his brother would try to jump me. "Fuck it…let'em try me." I psyched myself out. Adrenaline pumpin'! I went to gym ready to fight. As soon as I sat down on the outdoor basketball court—as was protocol for students so that the gym teacher could take attendance—the twin from my science class said to me, "so talk that shit now, punk."

I stood up. Looked at him dead in his eyes and invited him to attack me. All the students surrounded us—him in the front and his twin brother at my back.

He wanted to put on a show, so I'd give him one.

My blood was raging. And while she was gone, I heard my mother's voice telling little me to, "kick his ass." This time, not little Mitchell's, but these lame ass twins.

And that I did. I kicked both of their asses. Much to the shock of everyone in gym class.

"Damn, he beat both their asses."

In the process, I cracked my radius bone in my left arm because I was punching them with all my might. I'm left-handed and draw the strongest might from this arm. My dad, reluctantly, took me to the hospital the next day. My dad, the country-bumpkin that he was—given that he was born and raised in rural South Carolina—just thought the fracture would heal on its own. I wore a cast for a few weeks.

Of course, I got suspended! But during my week at home, I was all smiles.

This Black sissy could fight. And I knew this. I accepted this militant quality. This was the second time that I'd have to defend myself against more than one person at once—the first in fourth grade at Andrew A. Robinson. I beat them up, too: Michael and Hassan!

Nevertheless, I accepted the last suspension I'd ever have in school. I accepted my quiet warrior spirit and said to myself— fight like hell, David. Fight like hell.

From these fights, I developed a new mantra: *Underestimate me at your peril.*

5. Becoming a music-loving warrior sissy

Quietly, I was becoming not just a sissy but a warrior sissy who loved music. Through music and fighting, I developed newfound strength. I was also developing the confidence that I needed to survive the inner-city streets and their schools! I seeded this confidence quietly and over time, nurtured my then-budding warrior spirit with care, dignity, and love and a readiness to throw these hands without fear.

I would eventually, and finally, switch to the flute by eighth grade. By this time, though, I transferred from Eugene Butler Middle School to Twin Lakes Academy Middle (TLA). I transferred because Ms Milby was leaving Butler to serve as the Band Director at Twin Lakes, a brand-new magnet school located on the south side of town—the "rich" and "white" side of Jacksonville. She took Natoya and me with her. Well, we went through the magnet school lottery process, selecting TLA as our number one choice. We "won" our lottery! Indeed, we were students of TLA's first eighth grade class—class of 1998.

And the funny part? By that time, I had surpassed Natoya in playing the flute because for that year, in eighth grade, I landed 1st Chair and became "Section Leader," which pissed Natoya off and created tension in our friendship that lasted all throughout that year.

Our friendship only worsened when I auditioned for and was accepted into Douglas Anderson School of the Arts (DA)—a school that Ms Milby encouraged me to attend! Natoya went to the famed Mandarin High School and our bands were the top two in the District—which meant we were rivals. DA's Band was, by the judgment of District and State officiating, way, way better than Mandarin's band. Which meant that the players, like me, were far superior than those at Mandarin (though, they were, in fact, really good!). It took some years, but Natoya and I are far beyond the evil that competition created between us. She's lovely and without her, I would have never been in the band… and met *him*.

6. Him

Him. Oh god, him.

Brown skin, chipmunk cheeks with dimples, full thick lips, seductive smile, slightly taller than I, and a year ahead of me in school. He lived around the corner from me with his devoutly religious mother and two unequally yoked sisters. Often, I would stop by his house so that he could join me on my walk to school, to Butler. He was the best trumpet player in school. He was adored by all of his teachers, especially Ms Milby. He was respected by everyone. And even though he briefly dated Natoya, people suspected that he was gay. Hell, she did too!

On the first days of band class at Butler, when I sat to observe, I often found myself either daydreaming or actively searching the room—seeing if I knew anyone. I, as a sixth grader and, late comer, knew no one. Other than Natoya.

Then one day, I caught a glance of him. I'm sure he was unaware of me. I'd look away, or beyond, whenever he'd glance back at me. Yet, one day, I decided to wait for him to meet my gaze. It seems that on these days, he did his best to *not* look at me at all. But I didn't give up. I kept glancing. Staring. Rather, or not I irked his damn nerves, I don't know. But, on this particular day, he glanced back and our eyes locked in that moment. I smiled, coyly—he didn't. He just stared, like, "the fuck you lookin' at?" I didn't care. I blushed—though, I'm chocolate, so I'm not sure he could tell. After band class, he walked over to Natoya and they left class together.

After lunch, I struck up a conversation with Natoya, being noisy, of course.

"Oh, him. He's my boyfriend," Natoya tells me as we walked to Language Arts together.

Yep, she along with Charlotte, and I had Language Arts with Mrs Thomas, the same woman who accused me of threatening her.

"Oh, well that's cool…Ya'll look so cute together."

Yes, I was disappointed. But they were the perfect couple—everyone thought that.

I ended up talking to him one day, as friends, because by that time, I accepted that he was "straight." He and I hit it off immediately. He was funny, and he made me laugh. But more than anything, we shared a love for band. We were the ultimate band nerds.

Out of nowhere, he invited me over to his home so that we could practice. We practiced on his porch because his mother didn't allow his company inside her home. Whenever she looked at me, I sensed judgment. My effeminacy was blatant—I was obvious. Clock-able. I walked with a twist—and still do. My voice was soft. And still is.

His mother's religious devotion was also obvious. She made him attend church every Sunday and Wednesday—for bible study. And, chile, he knew that damn bible!!! So, no, I was never allowed in his home. And on the days that I randomly stopped by, she'd shout from inside her home—never ever greeting me at the door or her fence—"He ain't here." Somedays, I suspected that she lied.

Anyhow—

On the days he was home, we practiced and talked music for hours. HOURS. Even on the weekends, when I'd stop by and be greeted by his presence, he would whip out his instruments and play anything I asked. Yep, there were days that I would just sit and listen to him play—much to his and my delight.

On days that we walked to school together, he would speak of his dreams—what he wanted to be when he grew up. He spoke of his favorite bible characters and why he so much loved church. I'm sure I often tuned him out during these moments. By that time, I became suspicious of the church—who wants to be told that they are going to hell each Sunday? Every Easter, every Christmas?

Even after he and Natoya broke up, he and I remained good friends.

And we met on his front porch for much of my seventh-grade year—until…

"Two fucking faggots!"

Someone yelled this slur at us as we walked home from school one day and neared his front porch.

The next day, when I went to meet him at his home so that we could walk to school together, his mother came to the door and told me, rather curtly: "he already gone."

She did that the next day and the next day and the next day.

Soon, I stopped visiting him. Not because I wanted to. His mother told me that I was no longer allowed to visit him.

At school he avoided me.

He no longer met my furtive glances during band class. He even raised his music stand to block me out.

The school year ended. I transferred to Twin Lakes for eighth grade and he went on to high school.

He and I were over.

My heart.

Lorde my heart.

7. Douglas Anderson School of the Arts

"David, have you thought about where you want to go for high school," Ms Milby asked me one day after band class at Twin Lakes.

"Not really. Though, my sister Ann thinks that I should attend Stanton College Prep."

Stanton College Prep was the "it" high school in Jacksonville, where all the supposedly "smart" kids attended—especially if they were serious about going to college. Stanton was known for its Nationally Ranked IB Program[12] and my sister believed that attending Stanton would set me on the pathway to attending any college I wanted—even, Harvard.

However, Ms Milby offered a life-changing alternative.

"You should audition for Douglas Anderson."

"Douglas Anderson?"

"Yes. It's the School of the Arts here in Jacksonville. I think you should go there for music."

I had never heard of Douglas Anderson before. In fact, while I had started the process of applying to Stanton, I thought, truly, that I would go, like my sisters before me had, to my neighborhood high school: William M. Raines High School.

Curious, I asked Ms Milby for more information. She gave me the audition forms, which listed the dates of the auditions. At that time, there was only one audition left for the upcoming academic school year. *One.*

The audition requirements were, for me at least, rigorous: all twelve major scales by memory and a performance selection that displayed both technique and lyrical soundness. I had no fuckin' clue what any of this meant—lyrical soundness... what?!

I'd never auditioned for anything. Ever.

Luckily, I had enough time to figure out the performance selection. I knew the twelve major scales, thanks to my "five minutes a day" exercises. I just had to find something to play.

That something was de Georges Bizet's "2me Menuet De L' Arlésienne."[13]

Don't ask me how I discovered this piece. I was in eighth grade, I had no private musical training or teachers, and little did I know that I was performing what's consider in the Flute repertoire world a "master piece"—although a very dark master piece.[14]

Yet, somehow, this piece seemingly found me. I rehearsed this selection for hours, daily. After initially struggling to like it, I fell in love with the sound and feel of "L' Arlésienne." At some point, I stopped preparing it for DA and just started playing it from a deep place in my heart.

Whenever I played "L' Arlésienne," I reached for something in me that, at the time, I could not name. However, whatever I was after surely helped me to process my otherwise harsh and brutal realities.

I started to relieve the ache and pain of loss—of mother leaving. The sadness of losing a friend. The pain and hurt of being called a faggot, dirty, sissy all of my life. The hurt of sometimes not having food to eat. The shame I had of having to wear dirty clothes to school, or not having school supplies to start the school year. Through music, I began to massage a body that often lashed out to cope with the grief of being Black, gay, and despised by everyone.

Over the years, I now understand how in the sound of "L' Arlésienne," I found love—a love that I felt early in my childhood with mother. I found a softness. A quiet joy that I knew I had to protect and that no one could ever take from me.

On the day of my audition to attend DA, I was greeted by a white man, with a graying beard, and long pony-tail.

He introduced himself and asked me to do the same.

I said my name and told him of my performance selection.

I played the scales.

But, my dear, I sang Bizet.

All I could remember after my performance was he asking me: "Where did you get that tone from? It's like silk."

I shrugged my shoulders, thanked him for his gracious compliment, and quietly exited the room.

Days later, I received a voice recording from the school's librarian, Mrs Cherry—whom I also had my one-on-one interview with after my audition. She called to congratulate me on my acceptance into Douglas Anderson School of the Performing Arts.

I cried.

And of course, I accepted admissions into one of the best magnet schools in Jacksonville. That was Spring 1999. I entered in the Fall of 1999 and graduated from Douglas Anderson School of the Performing Arts with my High School Diploma and an Instrumental Music Arts Seal in May 2003.

But chile, guess what? Who did I see on the first day of my entry into high school school?!??!?!?!

Him.

6
Broken/ Hearted

Little did I know that the room where I auditioned for DA would be the room where I'd rehearse as a member of the school's orchestra. Next door was the home-room of the school's Concert and Symphonic Bands. As I entered the second room for band class, my heart stopped.

There he was. In the flesh, looking as good as ever.

And suddenly, I was flushed with both hurt and joy. Joy because of the sight of him. Hurt…well hurt because of how he just left me hanging.

I had no idea he attended DA. I had no idea what high school he attended after leaving Eugene Butler.

He really hadn't changed. Perhaps taller and a lil thicker, which made him delicious. The only real change was that he no longer played the trumpet in band. Instead, he played the clarinet and had, by that time, loudly embraced his Black queer self, without shame and with such joy.

It seemed that everybody at DA was gay—or something close to it! Really! Queer teachers, queer students, queer staff! Everybody! And although there are lots of stereotypes about queer kids in the arts, I relished in the climate and finally, once and for all, claimed my queer identity out loud, proudly, and joyously, too!

In claiming ourselves as Black and queer, together, we rekindled our friendship—and while there wasn't yet an explicit conversation about how we felt about each other, there was, in our immediately rekindling, fiery passion between us. Besides, it was wonderful to finally have a gay best friend, or something like that.

We went to dinner. Had date nights on the beach. We talked deeply about life. No more bible chatter (no, no!)...but about life. Our dreams, desires, wants. At school, we laughed and laughed and laughed! In between classes, we found each other and let the gaze we lost in middle school hold us in the five minutes we had to get to our next class.

Then one day, at school, sitting face-to-face in the courtyard:

"I'm so sorry," he says.

"For?"

"You know...how things went. You know...middle school."

I said nothing.

"My mom—she heard the faggot slur...and, well, she just wanted to keep me from you. She blamed you for bringing all that to her home. She said God condemns homosexuality."

"Me? What?"

He kept going on. I let him.

Then, suddenly, I spoke with what felt like rage. Certainly hurt.

"But you just stopped talking to me. You avoided me. You wouldn't look at me. You hurt me. I thought we were friends."

For a bit, all I recalled was him just staring at me. Saying little else, other than I'm sorry.

I'm sure I cursed his ass out—not appreciating at all his willingness to hold himself accountable for his once triflin' ass ways. I may have even slapped the shit out of him. My violent rages were sudden, unexpected, pent-up, and, when unleashed, deadly. Trauma and heartbreak can hold onto the soul for years, and when they converge and erupt, all hell can break lose.

He got up. Walked away. And this time I let him.

The next time we actively spoke to each other, a year later, he had a boyfriend.

The FUCK!?

He, now a junior, was dating a freshman.

Le sigh. No comment.

He and I had a toxic friendship since that moment, throughout, and after high school. We don't talk to this day and even as I narrate this heartbreak, I'm mad as hell at him.

Well, not really.

We just don't talk these days.

Prior to ceasing communication with him, we chatted here, chatted there. During these half-hearted, pass-aggressive, chinwags, he'd call to complain about whatever guy he was dating—or to share that he and so-and-so had just broken up. During one of these conversations, I asked him why he never chose me.

"You're too much. Plus, you got mad anger issues."

And before I could say or defend myself, he lands the *coup de grace*:

"Oh, you just too dark."

I said nothing and simply hung up the phone.

I imagine that after his repeated hellos, he finally heard, "if you'd like to make a call, please hang up and dial …"

Who cares.

At the end of the day, he said he just wasn't attracted to me. I was good enough to listen to his mess, but not good enough to date. I was good enough to be his rebound, when needed, and that was just about it.

He preferred dating "light-skin boys." And, looking back, his lil freshman boyfriend, in high school, was a "red-bone"—high yellow in color. His subsequent partners have all been white.

Because I'm petty, I deleted his cell phone number and blocked him on all social media.

It is what it is.

7
Black queer/ Lit

> I originally set out to write a story for me, because I realized I might be the only one who would read it. I wanted to write a story that would capture the pain and joy of being Black and gay. I wanted it to be a love story, because the one problem I had with admitting that I was gay was that I had to give up having true love like in the movies.
>
> —E. Lynn Harris, *What Becomes of the Brokenhearted*

The writer E. Lynn Harris is one of my favorite novelists. While he died in 2009, he single-handedly provided me with a literary survival guide for coming of age "Black" and "gay" in the south and, indeed, the inner-city. I discovered E. Lynn Harris because of "him." One day, it had to be a Saturday, I walked over to his house and, lo' and behold, he was sitting in his front yard reading a book.

"What are you reading," I ask him.

"*Abide with Me*," he says.

Because of his religious mother, and perhaps because of his own discretion, he hid the title and cover design of the novel with a brown paper bag that he crafted into a book cover. You see, the artistry and genius of Black kids in the inner-city is that we made beauty and art out of everything. Instead of buying one-dollar, brightly designed book covers, we simply re-used brown paper bags and created chic mono-chromatic, book jackets that were all the rave! Some folks even bedazzled them with glitter and magic markers!

Still though, in rather hushed tones, he told me that the novel was about Black gay men.

"WHAT?" I scream in dramatic high effeminate shock!

"Not so loud," he says.

By this time, he in tenth grade and me in ninth grade, we were pretty sure that we were gonna be gay in this life time. Though, we disclosed our gayness with each other at school—DA-- we didn't live as gay boys at home, in the hood. Discretion for him, I magine, but for us both a fear of…. *everything*.

At his mention of Black gay men, I became excited! I just had to get my hands on that book, so I etched the name E. Lynn Harris into my memory and began searching for his name during my weekend trips to my neighborhood public library—the Dallas James Graham Branch.

"The Graham," as I called it, still remains located across the street from Stanton College Prep high school, the school that my sister, Ann, hoped that I'd attend. The library also sits off Myrtle Avenue—the road that my mother once walked as a child in search of her own mother.

Whenever I visit Jacksonville, I stopped by the Graham. I'd walk in, observe, and then find a place to sit and close my eyes. I'm sure, to onlookers, I looked like a complete basket-case. However, in these meditative moments, I'd close my eyes and remember all the ways that this library provided me peaceful sanctuary. Sanctuary against the city's s summer heat; shelter from neighborhood violence that always lurked; and, equally important, a safe-space where I could relish in my joy of reading.

Figure 12 Jacksonville Public Library, Graham Branch. Jacksonville, FL. Picture taken December 27, 2024.

Nevertheless, a few days after leaving his house I went to the library hoping to find E. Lynn Harris. Of course, in her helping me search for E. Lynn Harris on the library's electronic catalogue, the Black woman librarian, with her ever-so-gentle face and judging eyes, shared the search results with me. "'These such books' were not at this public library," she said without ever looking at me, eyes glued to the screen and voice rather muted. And neither was I old enough to check out "these such books" without parental consent. I'm certain that my mother would have, had she been there, provided the librarian consent without many questions. My father? Chile, he would have gagged honey, choking and spittin' on his chewin' tobacco and all!

Still though, just as he did with me getting my first flute, my father, David Sr, played a huge role in me getting my hands on Harris' novels. Each Friday, when he got paid, he gave my sister Devita, lil brother Eric, and me five dollars; and if my daddy was feeling *really good*, then ten dollars. Instead of spending all of my money at the local Burger King or McDonald's, where I'd go with my sister and lil bother, I saved a few dollars here, a few dollars there. One Saturday morning, I woke up, spoke to hardly any one, and walked my lil happy Black gay ass all the way downtown to B-Dalton Book Store—crossing Myrtle Avenue and all—to purchase any book by this E. Lynn Harris guy.

The walk took about an hour and on pure adrenaline, I enter the book store, perhaps sweating, perhaps thirsty, but with a focused determination.

"Can you please tell me where I can find E. Lynn Harris?"

The white bookstore clerk gave me a look-over, judging me of course—probably because I didn't say "hello," a slight that can piss any southerner off. But honey, he knew my heart!

A quick clicking of the computer's keyboard.

"This way," he gripes.

Walking toward the back of the book store and past new and popular releases in African American fiction that were all fantastically displayed on book-case enclosures—Terry McMillan's *How Stella Got Her Groove Back*, Eric Jerome Dickey's *Sister Sister*, Omar Ty'ree's *Flyy Girl*, and Sister Soulja's debut novel *The Coldest Winter Ever*, which my sister, Hattie, and just about everyone on the block was reading—I arrive at the "H" section.

Shortly after the clerk leaves me, I glance over the books and without ever knowing that there was an order to reading E. Lynn Harris' novels, or without reading any of the novels titles, I just–by glancing at the pictures alone–picked up the book that I felt called to me the most.

Abide with Me

Ironic, right?

Hardly.

You see, I didn't know what the cover of this novel looked like. After all, he, my dear friend, had hidden the title and any images with his brown paper bag book cover. And, all the Black librarian told me in the Graham was that the library didn't carry "these such books."

So, with little pretense I purchased *Abide with Me*. Afterwards, knowing the error of my earlier misstep, I thanked the bookstore clerk, wished him well and left B-Dalton and the book clerk's smile, behind me. I didn't go straight home though. I headed for the Jacksonville Landing, an entertainment venue then located a few blocks from the bookstore. I purchased something to eat from Sbarro Pizza and sat in a quiet area and started reading *Abide with Me*.

Hours went by. Yet in no time, I discovered, for the first time ever, a world where not only Black gay and bisexual men existed but that they were also beautiful, sexy, fell in love with each other and, most of all, had something in common with me: fear, heartbreak, and yet a yearning for more: success.

With absolute delight, I finished the novel by nightfall and was hooked!

I'd soon consume as many of E. Lynn Harris' novels as I could. I'd read them, finally, in order: *Invisible Life (1994)*, *Just as I Am (1995)*, *And This Too Shall Pass (1997)*, *If This World Were Mine (1998)*, and, once more, *Abide with Me (1999)*. By the time I completed high school, in 2003, I'd read all of Harris' then published novels: *Not a Day Goes By (2000)*, *Any Way the Wind Blows (2002)*, and *A Love of My Own (2003)*. And most beautifully, my sister Hattie and I began discussing together how dramatic the characters were. Basil, the down low hunk of Harris' first three novels, was one of our favorites. "Chile, ain't he a mess," my sister Hattie once said to me.

"Hmmmhm… a fine damn mess at that," I'd say to her, before erupting in laughter.

From Harris' Black gay world, I began developing my own Black queer literacies; literacies that forever altered how I viewed and enjoyed myself as a Black queer teen coming of age in a world that doggedly tried to write me off, kill my spirit, and murder my soul.

Because of E. Lynn Harris, I was reminded of my love for reading—a love I almost lost as a result of the vicious, mostly white English teachers, I encountered in high school. Yet, given the times of our now, I also must note the vital importance of including "these such books" in school curriculum and libraries. Contrary to attacks on LGBTQ writers vis-a-vis book bans enacted by politicians, and particularly conservative legislators, Black queer books are life-saving. I don't know where I'd be without them.

This chapter, then, is a love song to Black queer writers and the voice they gave me to name and eventually survive the spirit murder that: one, defined my experiences within high school English classes *and* two, nearly derailed my pursuit of higher education.

Let's start with high school.

1. Douglas Anderson and summer reading

Douglas Anderson School of the Performing Arts has long prided itself on academic excellence. DA—as we affectionately referred to the red-brick school that sits nestled behind Phillips Highway and on the edge of the San Marco Neighborhood of Jacksonville, Florida[15]—was, in 2002, recognized by the US Department of Education as a National Blue-Ribbon High School.[16] Additionally, given its reputable arts-based curriculum, DA has received awards from the National Recording Academy of Arts and Sciences! For these reasons, educators and policy makers laude DA; and more, hundreds of students audition for entry, yearly. Lastly, DA remains the only performing arts high school in Jacksonville, which, to some, makes it an exceptional educational institution—that, and the high school is one of few named after a local African American civil rights activist.

Throughout their matriculation, DA students must balance their academic classes with a demanding arts education curriculum. Demanding because the arts curriculum, especially the Music program, prepares students to attend, as many have, colleges and universities like the famed Julliard School, Stetson University, and Eastman School of Music. I, once, dreamed of attending Julliard!

In preparation for academic study, each student must complete "summer reading." On the first days of school—no literally, the first day!!!—we'd have an exam on the summer reading, a select novel or two. Thanks to my beloved sister, Ann, I completed all "advanced" classes in eighth grade, at Twin Lakes Academy Middle School. Thus, during my matriculation at DA, each summer I read novels from the Honors English lists.

I enjoyed my summer reading and looked forward to entering the imaginative world of the "literary greats." For ninth grade, I read Ernest J. Gaines' *A Gathering of Old Men* and for tenth grade, Mary Shelly's *Frankenstein*. For eleventh grade, English III Honors, I read the two required novels: Sandra Cisneros' *The House on Mango Street* and Mark Twain's *The Adventures of Huckleberry Finn*. I say "required" because for both ninth and tenth grade, we could select a novel from a very short list of options. For Advanced Placement (AP) English, my senior year, I read Barbara Kingsolver's *The Poisonwood Bible* and Richard Wright's *Native Son*. Though long as hell, I loved both novels and screamed in angst over the social and economic plight of Bigger Thomas, Wright's central character in *Native Son*.

The cruelty of my experience with spirit murder began, though, at the start of my junior year, in English III Honors.

2. *Can You Come to My Desk?*

"David Green, can you come to my desk?"

During the middle of completing our Summer Reading Exam, my eleventh-grade English teacher summoned me to her desk.

Because the room was very quiet—we were, after all completing our exam—I could hear my heart beating outside my chest. Uncertain of why I was being summoned by the teacher, whose tough reputation preceded her, I approach and ask, timidly:

"Yes?"

She called me to her desk because she was curious about the vocabulary that I used in my summer reading essays, which, again, addressed *The Adventures of Huckleberry Finn* and *The House on Mango Street.*

"I've read your essays and I just have a few questions for you."

"Okay."

"Can you tell me what innocuous means?"

"Harmless."

"And blatant?"

"Obvious."

I didn't miss a beat in replying to her because as soon as she started her quizzing, I was, somehow, ready to play the game—the long game of dealing with white teachers that began way back at Eugene Butler Middle School.

She then asked me if I had written the essays myself.

The voice in my head went off!

Did this lady, who I don't know from a can of beans, just accuse me of cheating?

Yes, I printed my essays out on purple stationery because I didn't have any white paper at the place I was staying at the time. Yes. I wrote these damn essays and spent days "perfecting" every word, sentence, and idea.

Should I, a Black gay boy from the hood, not know "big words?"

Should I, a Black gay boy, enrolled in English III Honors, not know how to write?

What do I, the only Black boy enrolled in this section of her class, do or say to this white woman?

"Yes, I wrote the essays," I eventually answer.

"Are you sure?"

Bih---

"Yes, I'm sure."

Though close to doing so, I didn't curse. I didn't yell. I spoke with a level of calm I didn't realize was in me until that very moment.

There was a brief period of silence before she handed me back my essay. First, she inked in the grade: "A-."

Sitting down back at my desk, I read her comments in the right margins of my essay, words that I'll never forget.

Either you're a really good

writer, or

someone else wrote this for you.

Her handwriting was elegant and even beautiful as it appeared slanted, tilted to the left, in a unique and distinct cursive-like writing. But her words were the ugliest I'd ever read in response to my writing.

Both ashamed and embarrassed at the accusation that I cheated, and horrified that I was berated in front of my classmates—whose eyes I could feel burning my back—I did my best to hold back my tears as I tried to complete the Summer Reading Exam. I could not complete the exam because although *The House on Mango Street* was the novel I least understood at the time, it was the exam questions that I truly didn't understand. They were both poorly written and overly written. I hardly answered any of them, tears be damned.

I failed the exam.

Next to the big fat "F" were again violent comments by my teacher. "How could you do so poorly on the exam if you wrote the essays you claimed to write?"

I struggled all year in that lady's class. Switching into a different class with a different English teacher was not an option because doing so would admit defeat and give this woman more power that she already had (and lorded) over me. Besides, I was so ashamed of what my family would think of me; mostly because by that time, I was the "smart kid" who attended Douglas Anderson—the school of the artistically gifted. The Blue Ribbon School. So, I just sat silently in her class all year. Not really caring. Fearing she would publicly scold me. However, my fear manifested itself soon enough. In the middle of my presenting research on Quaker Culture and fascism, she scolded me without mercy. I pronounced fascism *"face-ism,"* to which she interrupted, "Excuse me, are you trying to say *fah-chism*?" After meeting her evil eyes with my own and letting her dismissive and hissing tone hang in the air before dissipating, I moved on, missed pronunciations and all. Nope, I did not answer her question at all.

I'm sure I got an "F" on that presentation and project—despite me spending hours and a few weekends conducting research at the Graham.

I earned straight "D's" in her class. I suspect that her progressive white-lady guilt didn't allow herself to fail me. At the end of the school year, however, she refused to advance me to AP English.

"You're just not ready nor capable."

I forged my guardian's signature on the placement forms and completed AP English my senior year. In the end, I was *the only* student in my class who *aced* the multiple-choice end-of-year final exam, which was on Toni Morrison's novel *Beloved*.

When my AP English teacher came to my name on the roster, she asked, like she'd done with all the students before me, if she could say my exam score aloud.

Yes, I tell her.

"100."

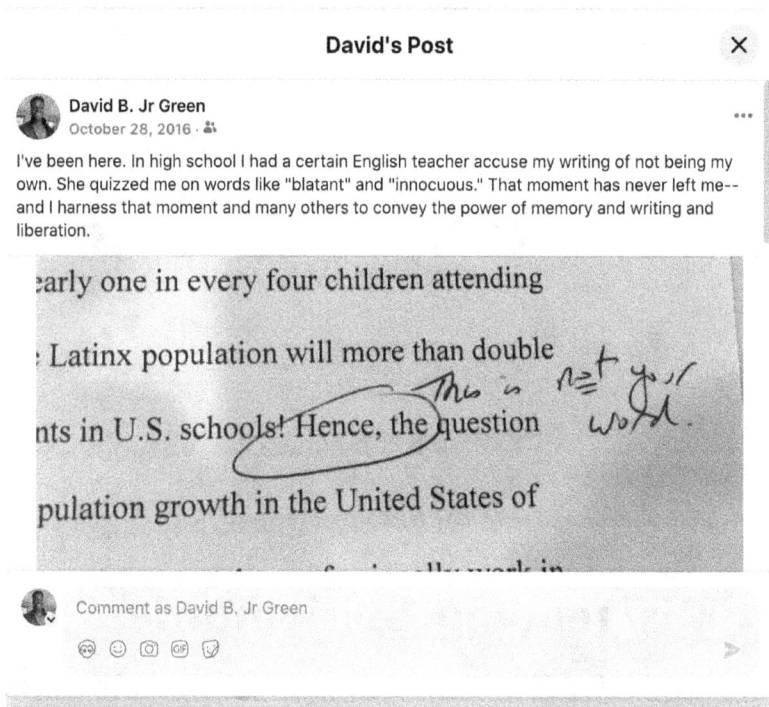

David's Post   ×

David B. Jr Green
October 28, 2016 · 🔏   ...

I've been here. In high school I had a certain English teacher accuse my writing of not being my own. She quizzed me on words like "blatant" and "innocuous." That moment has never left me-- and I harness that moment and many others to convey the power of memory and writing and liberation.

early one in every four children attending

Latinx population will more than double

nts in U.S. schools! Hence, the question   *This is not your word.*

pulation growth in the United States of

Comment as David B. Jr Green

Figure 13 Part 1. Screenshot of a Facebook Post I made that reflected my experience with my English III Honors Teacher. Screenshot Date: January 1, 2025.

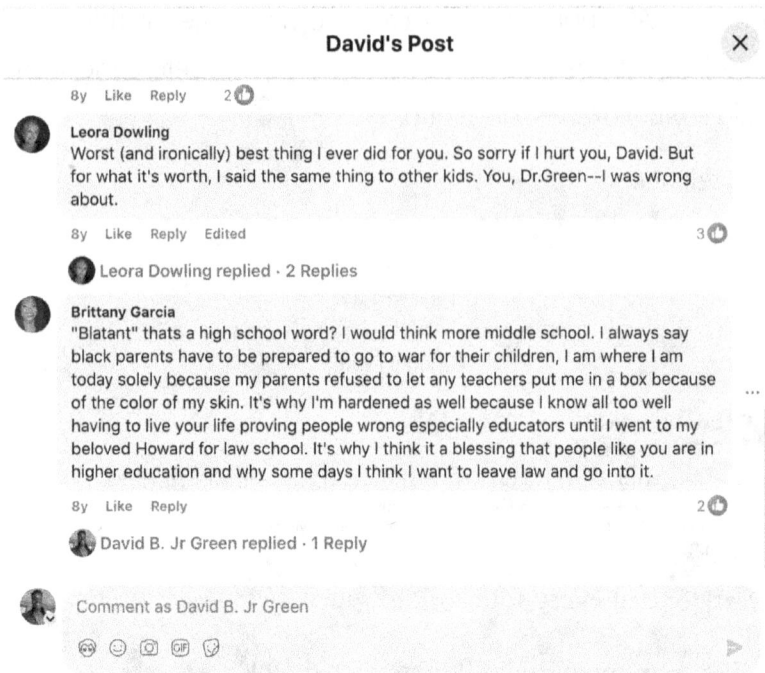

Figure 14 Part 2. Screenshot of a Facebook Post I made that reflected my experience with my English III Honors Teacher. Screenshot Date: January 1, 2025.

3. Mis/ reading. Spirit murder

English was one of my favorite subjects in school but I never told anyone—science and math were the others. I've always enjoyed entering fictive worlds where people's heroism triumphed over evil. I didn't have the language, courage, or tools to be a hero myself. And while I enjoyed Hester Prynne, of Nathaniel Hawthorne's *The Scarlet Letter,* the most that year during English III, I vowed not to ever publicly care or engage with English literature after high school. I'd simply go through the motions of jumping through whatever hoops necessary to finish the class, semester, and school year. The fear of humiliation was too real—the scars, too deep.

Throughout high school and college, I was often told by English teachers and professors that I mis-read passages, or, in the context of graduate school, that my "reading" was simply *wrong* or *too celebratory*. As a result, I internalized that I, somehow, "couldn't read" or that my scholarship was bad. I knew that I was not illiterate but somehow my comprehension and interpretation of literature and approaches to academic writing were inherently wrong. Something was wrong with me. I was intellectually defective.

How was this true when I really enjoyed reading? Despite what the "no child left behind generation" of teachers presumed about the literacy capabilities of Black youth and our joy of reading, I, in the privacy of my home, prepared for English exams through exuberant performances, a sort of spoken word style of study.

Many times, I often delighted, or perhaps tortured, my sister, Ann—and her then husband—with my reading of "Annabelle Lee," by Edgar Allen Poe. If it was not this haunting poem that I prepared for my oral presentation in English I Honors—with the infamous Mrs. Parker!-- then it was Poe's short story "The Raven;" or, for English II Honors, poems by Emily Dickens—and especially my favorites, "Tell all The Truth But Tell It Slant," and "Success is Counted Sweetest." Yet, somehow, and by the judgment of my English teachers, like "the purple host" spoken by Dickens in "Success is Counted Sweetest," "I 'could ne'r succeed."

Often, at school, in English classes, I remained silent. Afraid.

I've since learned that what I suffered from in my encounters with white English teachers is what education psychologist Claude Steele calls "stereotype threat."[17] In my silence, I feared confirming the "negative stereotypes" that white teachers held about Black intelligence. That I, and all Black students, lacked intellectual proficiency… *and* that we were (and are) inherently dumb.

Yet, stereotype threat represents only half the truth of my discovery. The violence of perpetually labeling my interpretation of literature as a "mis-reading," along with the harsh treatment by my English teachers was, in fact, me enduring for years what critical race theorist and legal scholar Patricia Williams call "spirit murder."[18]

Spirit murder wounds the mind. Spirit murder kills the belief and absolute joy that you have when engaging in something like reading. Spirit murder is the absolute ripping out of the heart by those who lorde their hatred and racial animus over you. Those who desperately want to see not just your absolute failure but your complete and total demise.

While both stereotype threat and spirit murder followed me throughout my undergraduate studies, they became nearly unbearable as I pursued graduate studies across two midwestern cities.

"Your writing is terrible," said one queer male faculty of color, who was then serving on my thesis committee.

"That's not trauma. What you experienced was not trauma," said one woman of color faculty, who was then serving on my thesis committee. I thought that I could—given that she was a woman of color faculty who survived higher education's racial and gender oppression—confide in her about my experiences as a graduate student of color and that she would understand and help. She didn't.

The trauma that she invalidated was in fact an experience that I had with two straight male faculty of color who called me into their office, shut the door, and berated me. In their judgment, I was far behind the other history students in the seminar. From their view, my discussion posts were too short and not long enough like the other students. I did not say much in class, and according to them, I was too silent.

Each of their verbal assaults came fast, one after the other. After what felt like an academic lashing, I left their office and did not enroll in another history class while completing my doctorate. I kept that promise.

Spirt murder came in the form of receiving an email notifying me that I did not receive a summer fellowship.

"Excuse me, but I *did not* apply for that fellowship," I reply to Leen, the Department's Graduate Student Coordinator.

Spirit murder was an entire department pulling the rug out from under my feet and in the process refusing to support me any further than required. Telling me "No" was on auto reply for them.

Spirit murder is a white male Department Chair yelling at me for not getting *his* permission to go home, after learning that my brother was murdered down in Jacksonville the day before.

No worries, after reading his email demanding that I stay and complete my Teaching Assistant (TA) duties as charged—it was the first week of classes—I politely got my ass up out of my office chair, walked down to his office, and—unlike the time when I stood in front of my English III teacher—went off on his ass… and went home, still.

He didn't believe in me anyhow. None of them did. None of them thought me capable.

4. Do you know who James Baldwin is?

Yet, and still, the most beautiful part about all of this ugly was that I was reading literature by Black queer writers. Lorde, they were my saving grace because before discovering a trove of Black queer writers, I nearly dropped out of graduate school twice. TWICE.

Before attending graduate school, I knew that I wanted to study Black gay people's lives, histories, and cultures. And while I will speak more pointedly about the McNair Program in the next chapter, I will say this now: If the McNair Program at the University of Florida (UF) provided me anything materially or substantially, then it was—beyond developing sound research methods—the knowledge that I wanted to know more about myself as Black *and* gay. Yeah, I enrolled in Black Studies courses, but they hardly mentioned Black gay people. My McNair research addressed the motivations for Black men attending college, but *I myself* hardly discussed Black gay men. Then, one day after my "Research Methods" class, the professor, Dr Stephanie Y. Evans asked me if I planned to attend graduate school. I tell her yes, sure, and before she could ask about my research interests, I blurted out that I wanted to study Black gay people. She followed up my declaration with, "Do you know who James Baldwin is?" I didn't and to my not knowing she quipped, "David, you cannot call yourself a Black gay man if you don't know who James Baldwin is."

Her words were precise and motivating. I'd head to the bookstore in search of James Baldwin. I found his first novel, *Go Tell It on the Mountain*, and didn't understand a single word. Then I found, months later, Baldwin's *The Fire Next Time* and *chilllleeee*. It was like talking to a Black gay uncle who had had enough of white people, the Black church, and America's racism. Woo, honey, if only I could write and think like Baldwin! Mercy!

Mimicry aside, my courage to speak boldly was brewing in my soul and for the next several years throughout my graduate studies and research, I mined Black queer archives at the Schomburg Center for Research in Black Culture, in search of something like freedom. With the help of Steven Fulwood, who curated the Schomburg's Black Gay and Lesbian Archive, freedom's horizon was emerging quite beautifully.

Black queer history and writers fed my soul. And thanks to the then emerging field of Black Queer Studies, I could theoretically situate Black queer writers for the purpose of writing my dissertation.[19] A deep joy, though, was reading the poems, short stories, novels, and plays written by people who looked and lived like me.

Thus, when the hate machine of graduate school became unrelenting, I emersed myself in Black queer literature. In, with, and through their words, I could feel their love. In, with, through their words, I learned how to deal with the pain of rejection…and the devastation wrought by those who simply hated Black gay people.

I was not defective and while I interpreted literature differently than expected by teachers and their anti-Black, euro-centric standards, I was not mis-reading anything. I didn't need to be like the other history students to be me. And I most certainly didn't need a white man's permission to attend my brother's gawtdamn funeral! And and and! I would no longer take shit from professors who refused to see the beauty and genius of Black LGBTQ people and our histories! PERIOD!

Indeed, my people, the Black Queer Ancestors, saved my soul and guided my heart. Nobody, and I mean not a single damn person, was gonna turn me around.

While many Black queer people were rejected by friends, family, their churches, and organizations, they often turned inward to each other and internally to their own souls.

Although people hardly believed in Black queer people:

Still, they danced.

Still, they sang.

Still, they wrote.

Still, they gave us the Harlem Renaissance.

Still, they gave us the Stonewall Rebellion.

Still, they gave us Black Feminism and Womanism (and the Color Purple).

Still, they gave us Black Pride.

Still, they

Spoke

The "ass-splitting" truth,

With

Eloquent thunder.[20]

And, finally, you see, I found the words to do so myself. I defended my doctoral dissertation on my late brother's birthday and earned my PhD in August 2015.

5. Discovering Audre Lorde

I survived stereotype threat and spirit murder because of Black queer writes, indeed, and most certainly because of the Black lesbian feminist poet and mother: Audre Lorde. My fear of engaging with words, in any space or place, changed forever after I discovered Lorde's life and writings.

On a trip to the University of Maryland Baltimore County (UMBC) to attend a Ronald E. McNair's Scholars Conference, I sat in a presentation where a fierce young Black queer woman scholar, Rachel Dudley, delivered a presentation on Audre Lorde—whom before this moment, I'd never heard about.

In this presentation, Rachel performed an electrifying reading of Audre Lorde's poem, "A Litany for Survival." Please abide with me as I quote this poem in its entirety. My greatest hope is that you take a piece of this poem with you in the name of love, healing, and joy.

Lorde's, "A Litany for Survival," reads:

For those of us who live at the shoreline
standing upon the constant edges of decision
crucial and alone
for those of us who cannot indulge
the passing dreams of choice
who love in doorways coming and going
in the hours between dawns
looking inward and outward
at once before and after
seeking a now that can breed
futures
like bread in our children's mouths
so their dreams will not reflect
the death of ours;
For those of us
who were imprinted with fear
like a faint line in the center of our foreheads
learning to be afraid with our mother's milk
for by this weapon
this illusion of some safety to be found
the heavy-footed hoped to silence us
For all of us
this instant and this triumph
We were never meant to survive.
And when the sun rises we are afraid
it might not remain
when the sun sets we are afraid
it might not rise in the morning
when our stomachs are full we are afraid

of indigestion
when our stomachs are empty we are afraid
we may never eat again
when we are loved we are afraid
love will vanish
when we are alone we are afraid
love will never return
and when we speak we are afraid
our words will not be heard
nor welcomed
but when we are silent
we are still afraid
So it is better to speak
remembering
we were never meant to survive.[21]

All I could hear in Lorde's poem was being alone, being afraid, not speaking, and being silent. In Lorde's poem, I read clearly my own fears, and I was shaken by them. It's why I emphasize the line:

and when we speak we are afraid
our words will not be heard
nor welcomed

On those occasion that I mustered the courage, I tried my best to speak truthfully in my writing and class discussions. My speaking was met with condemnation because people refused to hear the joy in my voice, nor take seriously the value of Black queer life.

"Can you talk about anything other than black gayness?"

"Talking about yourself, self-referentially or autobiographically, does not account for real research."

"Your research is too celebratory."

I would leave UMBC renewed and on a search to find Audre Lorde. Shortly after we McNair scholars landed in Gainesville (Florida), I headed to Barnes and Noble, and this time, I found Lorde without any assistance from a store clerk. I picked up *Sister Outsider*, Lorde's essays and speeches, and devoured every word. *Sister Outsider* now serves as my bible and whenever I'm in doubt or in need of inspiration, I turn to Lorde's words to find my voice.

In *Sister Outsider*, Lorde asks: "Of what had I *ever* been afraid?"[22] I applied Lorde's question to my own life. What had I ever been afraid of? Yeah, I sounded/ sound like a girl, walked/ walk like a girl, was poor, am Black, and am dark skinned, and was often met with violence, hate, and disregard. But does that mean I have to hate myself? Quiet myself? Nearly disappear myself in the harshest of moments?

In retrospect, before reading literature by Black queer writers, I used my silence to "hide myself." As the Black lesbian poet Pat Parker writes in her poem "Have you Ever Tried to Hide," I used my silence in an attempt to "slide between the floor boards." Slide myself "away from [the classroom]," before teachers noticed my "Black self" with their "white minds" or for some, their "straight" minds.[23]

After I discovered Audre Lorde specifically, and Black queer writers broadly, I no longer hide through silence. Like the Black lesbian poet and writer Cheryl Clarke does in her essay, "New Notes on Lesbianism," I name myself, Black, queer, and free.[24]

For the rest of my college years, and most assuredly as a graduate student, I made a promise to myself: to live from a space of freedom, love, joy, and honesty. I moved away from all that I was afraid. Inspirited by Lorde's poem, I made a vow to myself: I would become, despite being accused of mis/ reading and shunned so profoundly by otherwise "progressive teachers," that which I've always wanted to be: *a Black Queer Teacher*.

8
From the hood to the hooded/ Black Queer Teacher

I believe the children are our future,
Teach them well and let them lead the way
Show them all the beauty they possess inside
Give them a sense of pride

—Whitney Houston, "Greatest Love of All"

Listen as your day unfolds
Challenge what the future holds
Try and keep you head up to the sky
Lovers, they may cause you tears
Go ahead, release your fears
Stand up and be counted
Don't be ashamed to cry

—Des'ree, "You Gotta Be"

When I was not that little boy running away from bullies, on my way home to Apartment 24, in Palm Terrace, I would often sing Whitney Houston's, "Greatest Love of All." For whatever reasons,

I reached for that song, and sang to myself as I sat with my legs in between the spaces of the iron, rusting, banisters.

I'd start singing the opening lines quietly.

> *I believe the children are our future*
> *Teach them well and let them lead the way*
> *Show them all the beauty they possess inside…*

But, by the song's midpoint, the timbre of my singing would increase and more audibly, I'd belt:

> *I decided long ago,*
> *Never to talk in anyone's shadow*
> *If I fail, If I succeed,*
> *At least I'd lived as I believe*
> *No matter what,*
> *They take from me*
> *They can't take away my*
> *Dig-na-teeee*[25]

I just loved that moment of the song. I felt powerful singing to myself—words and expressions that I'm sure I didn't understand but somehow moved my lil Black boy spirit.

I'd sing that song as much as I could before someone eventually called me into the house to do something.

But that was my song, and it really got me through some rough times.

Over the years, I've come to understand the spiritual significance of "Greatest Love of All" and why its lyrics spoke to me so deeply. At its heart, "Greatest Love of All," spoke about not just love but believing in the power of love. Believing in the power of love requires that I, you, and we do all that we can so that our everyday actions lead to creating spaces and places were all people can survive, thrive, and live with joy. For me, my love for school allowed me to develop, over the years, love in action; that action was becoming a teacher.

You see, I've always known that I wanted to be a teacher. I've always loved school. Yet, coming of age in the inner-city, all I've ever heard was that teaching is for girls, *real men don't teach*. They hustle and earn their coins in other ways, through other professions. Sport, music entertainment, or joining the military (and especially the Army) presented themselves as the most viable career options—these, or becoming a doctor or lawyer. Such careers seemed the most viable because, in fact, the 1990s was an overwhelmingly visual era. Television, music videos, movies, posters, and sports trading cards were all but a smattering of examples that collectively represented exciting career possibilities for young Black boys like us. However, teaching was not among the careers represented or marketed through the lens of Black manhood or masculinity.

The idea that men don't teach is a lie. Those that I encountered growing up were mostly white. However, like Mr J, of the Boys and Girls Club, Black male teachers have existed in and outside of the classroom. And—despite the historic low numbers of Black male teachers, our numbers are on the rise given pipeline organizations such as The Center for Black Educator Development.

Still though, even before I ever read about and studied the data on Black men who teach in America, Whitney spoke to me.

"Teach them well and let them lead the away/ show them all the beauty they possess inside/ give them a sense of pride."

As Whitney sang, she wrapped the lyric's prophetic powers around me—an embrace that has never let go.

I'm living my dream and have indeed achieved "the greatest love of all," as Whitney sings, and became a teacher... not just any ole teacher, but a Black Queer Teacher.

This chapter is a love song to that becoming.

A love song to never giving up.

A love song to not ever letting anyone kill your dreams or murder your spirit.

And, more importantly—

A love song to help those coming up behind you keep their dreams alive, too.

1. Black queer boy at play

You may be wondering, dear reader, how might a young boy, barely himself in school, know what he wants to be when he grows up?

One answer could be this: at Bethune Elementary we kiddos were often asked what we wanted to be when we grew up. On career days, DARE Officers—when they were not promoting their JUST SAY NO TO DRUGS campaign—were, like most guests, inquiring about our future lives. School officials and guest speakers alike worked overtime to adult us Black kids. They worried less about play and the emotional enrichment of playing, and more about readying our bodies for labor.

Another answer, and one that taps into the creative genius of Black kids, is this one:

I played school!

Yep, I played school with my sister, Devita—who once dreamed of becoming a lawyer—and sometimes alone with imagined students. I'd pretend to teach lessons that I had learned in school. I'd write 1+1 = ____ and I asked my student or students to provide the answer. Or, I would write A, B, C and say, what letter comes next?

And I played school well past the time that I should have stopped; well past elementary school. Well past middle school. For various family members, I helped them prepare for exams by creating practice exercises. I'd read through their lessons and create spelling tests, math quizzes, and vocabulary tests—which included oral exams. I'd grade them as if it were the real deal.

> *Yes, that' right*
> *or*
> *no, that's wrong.*
> *This is the right answer*

I was always a kind teacher determined to make sure my students/ cousins/ siblings learned their lessons. I'd show my students/ cousins/ siblings steps to correct a wrong answer—and yes, sometimes, if the student/ cousin/ sibling acted up, I'd send them to time out.

> *Go sit in the corner.*

Black boys don't often get the chance to simply play—play for joy and perhaps without the spirit of competition that sometimes comes with pee-wee and junior football leagues.

Black boys can't always retreat to imaginative, creative spaces, out of luxury. We are called out as sissy when we/ our/ my expressivity becomes too much, too felt, or too seen.

When Black boys retreat to these creative spaces, we are, though, often escaping, running from something; running toward something.

For me, I was running away from the pain, yet running toward that which I truly loved. While I was playing, I was connecting with people. I saw their frustrations with learning. How they began to internalize beliefs that they were incapable.

In those moments, I leaped into action and responded to them with care. I gave pieces of my own broken heart in an effort and hope to mend their own. When my students—who were, by middle and high school, more than just my sister but extended family—began to understand their assignments, my own convictions of teaching grew stronger. Their joy helped cure me, too—each moment of joy helped to chip away at my own pain and brokenheartedness.

I was developing, or had something in me (call it innate), a practice of care deeply rooted in my own vernacular—grounded in my own intimate racialized experience with literacy (in)justice. As I look back to those years, I see that my engagement was also organic. In this way, I was bridging together my experiences with those who I "taught," and discovered in the process that they, too, were hurt by society. They, too, were aching to be more, to feel more, and to somehow carve out a sense of *more-ness* through education.

After each play, or tutor session, I would lock those moments in my heart and take them with me whenever one door closed— or, more precisely, when I'd have to leave or was put out of one home.

Even as I played school, housing insecurities followed me. But during a most serendipitous chance meeting, something beautiful happened that led to building a life-long sturdy bridge—a bridge that helped pave the way to my becoming a Black Queer Teacher.

2. Lucky: My godmother

As a Black Queer Teacher, I aim to restore and help students (and people) *feel* again. To restore that emotion, joy, and belief that was lost and stolen by the ghost of injustice…and hatred.

Let it be known, though, that I did not become a Black Queer Teacher all on my own. There were people put on this earth who, before I could have ever predicted, were destined to be in my life. My three sisters—Ann, Hattie, Devita—most assuredly. Yet, there is also someone who I didn't meet until my middle school years, when my birth mom left for the second time. Someone who would, over time, and with great care and love, claim me as her son. This woman became my godmother. Her name? Lucky Latrail Perkins.

No seriously, her real, birth, name is Lucky and how fortunate was I to meet her. Ma'dea, as I've come to call her, after "mother dear," has been in my life since seventh grade. I met her one day on the front porch of my daddy's house. At the time, we were living at 1525 McConihe Street. The year was 1997, the same year that I discovered E. Lynn Harris and purchased *Abide with Me*, the first novel I read about Black queer folks!

Here is that story:

As I was practicing my clarinet, a black truck pulls up in front of our house. Inside the truck, a woman was honking her horn as she was blasting R&B music! Shouting at me from the driver's side, made audible because the window to the passenger door was down; she was asking me questions that I didn't understand.

She must have seen my face, which was like, "lady what?" As such, she turned down the volume of her music and asked again:

"Is Bunk in there?"

"Bunk? Yeah. Hol on."

I shouted through the tattered screened window that connected the front porch and the main living room. Bunk was in my daddy's room, which was also connected by a door to the living room. You can have whole loud ass conversations between the front porch and anyone in the front rooms.

"Buuunnnkkkkk," I shout dramatically, because chile it was summer time in Jacksonville—which meant that it was hot as hell and that I was not moving from in front of the fan!

"Huuuuuuh?" Bunk replies with even greater drama.

"Some lady out here askin' for you."

Out came Bunk in her typical attire—crop top, short-shorts, sandals—and she shouts:

"Laaaatraillllll."

Bunk was my dad's then girlfriend. She lived in a two-bedroom apartment around the corner on Ella Street but often stayed nights with my dad. Bunk was a tall, statuesque, Brown-sugar colored woman, with a beautiful near-perfect round baldhead. She wore halter top shirts and short shorts—daisy dukes—and sometimes wore pumps. She had a gold noise ring and an even *golder* tooth. She always smelled good and was, of the many women my dad dated, my favorite!! She was funny as all get out. She took her sometimes "live-in girlfriend" status seriously. She cooked, cleaned, and made sure "Green," as she called my dad, performed his fatherly duties. She is the reason why my daddy purchased me my first flute.

"Green dis boy need a damn flute. Go get him a damn flute."

After a brief back and forth, we got in my dad's long white car and drove to *The Music Man*. And just like that I had my flute.

"One thing for sure, two things for damn certain," she'd always say, "I'm not here to replace your mother. I got my own sons. But I love ya'll. Imma see it to whatever ya'll need ya'll get."

Bunk was also Lucky's sister—she was older than my godmother.

Once Bunk appeared on the porch, Lucky got out of her truck—a Toyota 4-Runner—and what a beautiful sight!

She was a darker shade of Brown-sugar than Bunk. She was much more voluptuous but presented herself just as fashionable as Bunk. She was decked out in gold jewelry. Her perfume reached me before she did. She too rocked a short haircut—whereas Bunk had no hair, Trail styled her short cut with bouncing curls.

And baby, her outfit was clean!!!! All I remember was a bunch of white—almost blinding white set off by the glistening gold jewelry.

Bunk introduced me with little fanfare.

"Trail, dis Green son."

And before I could say "hey, how you doin," as is southern custom, my godmother asked what felt like a million questions.

WhatisyourenameWhatschoolyougotowhatgradeyouinYoumakeg oodgradesHowlongyoubenplayingthatthereinstrumentBunktellme thatyoursmartYouacutelilchocolatethangYouwannaridewithus?

Hmmhmm—talk about sensory overload.

And talk about nosey!!!

I did ride with them though. We just rode around town before stopping to get something to eat. We then went back to her house and *OhMyGoodnessss!!!!!*

Her house was beautiful. A large, all-brick home located off Dunn Avenue and down Biscayne Boulevard in a recently built subdivision: *Biscayne Estates East*. And estates these were! Each home was brick, big, and had its own sprawling green, well-manicured lawn. This is where the "rich Black folk" lived. This neighborhood was very different from my own, and any that I'd lived in.

As we entered her house, she offered me ice cream and cookies. I'd soon meet her husband, Sammy, who became my god-daddy, and her two kids, Nate and Joy, my god brother and sister. I'd also meet more members of my new-found family. Cousin Ashley and her mother, Dee, were my new favorites! Dee was a real hoot with the most infectious, deep, baritone-belly laugh!

Anyhow, as time went on, my godmother nurtured my spirit for school. While she often wondered where my mother was, she never said a mean thing about the otherwise "woman who left her kids." Instead, like her sister Bunk, she met me with grace and love. She invited me to stay over at her house as many times as I'd like and more importantly, she allowed me to use the family's computer. This was the first time that I'd met a family who owned a computer. Again, in my eyes, these were rich folk!

Soon, she'd just come by my father's house to pick me up, for no other reason than to spend time with me.

"Hey boo! Need anything? Come on let's go!"

With my godmother, I found, for the very first time, someone I could laugh with and not be judged, or told "get out of grown folx faces."

Instead, she invited me to be myself.

"You gay baby?" It's okay if you are.

But her question read and sounded more like a factual statement.

"You gay, baby."

Indeed, I was but didn't say this to her then. Though, I came out to her by high school. We went clubbin' together. Her, Dee, and myself.

One day, while I was working on homework at the kitchen table-- at this time, I was in high school at Douglas Anderson—my godmother sat at the table to strike up a conversation.

She opened my History notebook and saw that I had an "A" on every assignment.

And I mean like A+, 105 here, 110 there.

"How you stay so focused on school given you know…"

I knew what she was getting at.

And I simply told her: "I just like school. Besides, my history class is easy."

School was indeed my escape. My safe place.

Then, after a bit of silence, she said something that inflamed my heart.

"You were born with so much favor. You know that? *God's* favor."

While I knew that my godmother attended church, this was the first time she shared her spiritual wisdom.

"God's favor?" I ask her.

This was the first time that anyone had ever associated me, a Black gay boy, positively with religion or spiritualism.

My godmother would go on to share that somehow God's plans for me was deep; that because of his love for me, I was somehow shielded against what felt like attempts by people to kill my spirit.

In that moment, I could not offer much in response to her— except a hug, a thank you, and that I loved her. However, that night, as I lay on the make-shift bed she always had ready for me, I started singing, without much thought, Whitney Houston's, "Greatest Love of All." Shortly after I started singing, it hit me! Now

I understood why that song resonated with me so deeply as a child. That spirit I felt all those years ago was God's.

I found God in myself and I loved her fiercely.[26]

3. Shots!

As I mentioned earlier in this story, my high school, Douglas Anderson, was a performing arts magnet with a renown reputation. The music program exposed students to exceptional music education that included members of the Orchestra, Jazz, and Symphonic Wind Ensemble traveling throughout Florida to perform at music invitationals. On one of the trips, I received a call from my godmother. She called to inform me that an envelope from the University of Florida had arrived addressed to me and called—yes called—to ask me if I wanted her to open it or not. I asked her about the size of the envelope because at the time, in the early 2000s, at least, large-sized envelopes typically meant that you were admitted into that university or college.

"It's regular size," she tells me.

My heart sank. I just knew that I was rejected and not offered admissions.

"Yeah, I say, go ahead and open it."

Silence. Because she was reading.

"You got in!! Congratulations you have—"

I just screamed.

My bandmates started asking me questions:

"Oh my goodness, what happened? What's wrong?"

"Oh nothing, I got into UF!"

I'd spent countless hours at my godmother's house, on the computer, writing my college admissions essays. So much so that my god sibs were gettin' aggravated that I was hoggin' all their time.

I was and for that I am so sorry!

I was denied by so many schools in Florida, but UF came through!

When I got home, back to my godmother's house, I read the letter myself—for proof, I guess.

The embroidered letters were metallic Blue, like the school's colors—which are orange and blue! And it was true, I was admitted. Shortly thereafter, an "Award letter" arrived. With a combination of grants, scholarship, and loans, my tuition was fully covered.

There was only a small stipulation: I was admitted into the AIM Program[27], which meant that I'd have to start school, if I accepted admissions, that summer 2003—a few weeks after my high school graduation. With little thought, I accepted admissions and was preparing for college!

With the great fortune of my godparents, I was preparing to start college. Yet on move-in day, I received a call from UF officials notifying me that they had not received my immunization records showing me having the latest tetanus and Hepatitis B shots. As a result, I could not move in the Residence Halls until they received proof of immunization.

Literally, the truck, that same black Toyota 4-runner, was packed to the brim with going to college wares. We went shoppin' shoppin' shoppin'—*Bed, Bath, and Beyond*, and *Wal-Mart Super-Center* (mainly for groceries)!

After telling my godparents the news, I was sad, devastated! However, my godparents didn't think twice and asked me to find the nearest location to get "shots."

The shots would be costly, well to me anyway. I didn't have any money. We located a place, on the north side of Jacksonville, and scheduled an immediate walk-in. Within the hour, I was boosted up and ready for college! We came back to my godparents' house, scanned a copy of the immunization card, awaited clearance from UF officials, and with a yes off we drove down I-10 to Gainesville, Florida!

We were all excited!

"See," my godmother says to me.

"Favor"

With the help of my godparents, I moved into Hume Hall. Bed made, food in fridge, and after a short observation of campus from my godmother…

"These white kids gone stay runnin'. I bet they ain't even moved in yet,"

we said our goodbyes. And just like that my godparents and aunt Dee, were off.

I sat in my room and thanked God for his favor.

4. AIM: TexasGatorGul

The University of Florida was hell—at least in the early days. I almost dropped out twice. The first near dropout resulted from an error in my financial aid records and led me to endure the grueling and cruel verification process. I had, on my FAFSA form, reported that my father served in the military—which he claimed he did. The school wanted proof of that—though, I'm not sure why—I was not receiving any veteran benefits!

Anyhoot, because I failed to verify my father's military status, my financial aid was yanked from me, which meant that I could not pay my housing bill. As a result, I was forced to leave the dorm, or be kicked out. I left and retroactively withdrew from the semester, after, though, having received D's in my classes—because I could not attend them in person. Do note that prior to leaving, I had A's in all of my classes!!! I was so ashamed to have had to return home to Jacksonville. But because I petitioned the school to withdraw from the semester, I salvaged my GPA and was permitted to return to UF for the Fall 2023 semester—and I did so with a vengeance!

Whew, honey! But I returned to a hostile social space! The summer semester was at least chill, relaxing, and peaceful. I returned that Fall to a climate of homophobia that shook me to my core. Indeed, I found that my Black queerness was not welcomed by many at UF—from professors to staff, to students—including the Black students. At every turn, I could hear laughter and jeers, whispers of "chile he gay, so sad." And I'm not even gonna say much about the white queer spaces. I followed the advice of Student Life professionals who suggested that participating in clubs could enrich the first year(s). I tried but my efforts were met with brutal, wholesale, social rejection; I experienced what I've come to learn as *unbelonginess*. I wanted to simply leave UF. I was lost and very lonely in those early years. Like I always did, I turned to writing and wrote a poem, "Silent Soliloquy" which won a

Black History Award and was published in some Black journal for expressive arts at UF.

Just as I was about to give up on this school thing, I met someone whose love, care, and vision for what's possible helped to alter the course of my academic trajectory. She was an RA, Resident Assistant, for Trusler Hall; the residence hall I lived in during my freshman year—I only lived in Hume Hall that previous summer. Her name was Joyce Olushola, and her AIM (AOL Instant Messenger) screen name was TexasGatorGul. She is from Texas and is proudly Nigerian (and super good at math!!!).

I sent her a message on AIM.

"Joyce, I don't think I'm returning to UF next year."

She told me to come down to her floor so that we could talk in person. We ventured over to the café that adjoins our residence all with the multipurpose space—study rooms, recreation, swimming.

She asked me what led me to feel that way, about leaving UF. I told her that I just don't feel as if I fit in. I didn't feel comfortable in my classes, where I was often one of few Black students. I didn't feel completely comfortable with the Black students, who often had something to say about me being gay and I didn't feel comfortable with most of the white students and their passive aggressive anti-blackness. My professors intimidated me and while I was supposed to receive mentorship from folks in the AIM program, my mentor just stopped showing up to our meetings. He was a Black male student—presumably heterosexual and later became a member of Alpha Phi Alpha, a Black Fraternity. I'm sure my being Black and gay made him uncomfortable. The Black Administrators in the AIM nor PAACT Program did not reach out to support me at all.

After listening to me, Joyce offered a solution.

"David, just give it one more year because there is a program that I think would welcome you. It's called the Ronald E. McNair Scholars Program. You can get a scholarship and do research. You just have to be in year three to meet eligibility requirements."

Joyce was, herself, a McNair Scholar.

After much hesitation, I bided my time. I even called Hampton University—a Historically Black University located in Hampton, Virginia—to withdraw all transfer paperwork. Yes maim, I was dead serious about leaving UF and called Hampton, where I was admitted a year prior, to ask about transferring.

That next year, I held to the promise of returning to UF with the hope of applying to the McNair Program within a year. I applied as soon as the application went live that Spring 2005 semester, and I was surprised to receive an interview.

I was interviewed by two Black women, Mrs Daniels and Dr Cochran—a professor of education or psychology (or both!)

Lorde, I'm so happy to have met them. During the interview, they welcomed me with such grace. We laughed, yes, and also engaged in deep conversation, inspired by provocative questions.

Not only was I asked the important question of:

"Why do you want to be in the McNair Program?"

But I answered the question:

"How would this program meet any life goals that you have for yourself?"

I cleared my throat and answered with as much confidence as I could:

"I want to find myself. As a Black gay man, I'm in search of me, a scholarly validation of me and people like me. Community, what is that? I don't know, but I hope I can find community in this program."

My responses to their questions were brief, but all I could do was tell the truth and speak from the heart.

Dr Cochran and Mrs Daniels just stared at me.

Shit, I was thinking. Well, there goes that. At least I tried.

Weeks later, I received an email notifying me that I was accepted into the McNair Scholars Program.

I cried, called Joyce, met her for lunch, hugged her, and thanked her for helping to save, restore, and revitalize my joy for learning and school.

I started the McNair Program the following summer and met Dr Evans, who as you already know, introduced me to James Baldwin months later. That year, indeed, at the McNair Conference at the University of Maryland—Baltimore Campus (UMBC), I discovered Audre Lorde and the rest is history. I was even featured in a campus news article[28] about my experiences as a McNair Scholar and have since delivered a Keynote Address to and for the program.

I applied to graduate school—a whole bunch of them. As a McNair Scholar, all of my application fees were waived, so why not. I received rejections from many schools but ultimately prevailed.

God's favor.

Figure 15 Invitation Letter to Deliver Keynote Address at McNair Banquet.

Figure 16 Me with Dr. Samesha Barnes, Director of the McNair Program and Ronda Marks Vincent, Administrative Assistant. We are celebrating the occasion and full circle moment.

5. Love: Being a Black Queer Teacher

I attended graduate school and earned my Master's Degree in African American Studies and PhD in American Studies. My academic pedigree is the result of love.

Lemme repeat and center:

my academic pedigree

and the degrees that I have earned in my life,

is the result of

love.

The love that I received from Black women, and all who believed in me—even at times when I didn't always believe in myself—lives within me deeply. Love is my spirit guide, my tool to fight against the multiple and intersecting injustice that Black queer people face and endure. My love's reach is deep, though, and is wide enough to wrap itself around anyone who will welcome my grace and anyone who needs love.

Love saved me from being a victim of circumstance. Love has given me voice. Love is my pedagogy and guides my teaching and professional development practice—I teach and lead with love in every instructional learning space that I enter, be it a class-room or a professional development enrichment session.

Learning to love can be hard. My experiences with teaching, lit-eracy, and learning in US schools and colleges in and beyond the inner city has taught me that if we welcome love and let it con-dition us, condition our soul, then we can learn to both welcome its presence and share out its power.

Love is, indeed, very powerful.

Receiving love, feeling its spirit, comes with, at least for me, a great responsibility.

As a Black Queer Teacher I see you, Black queer child. Person. Friend. I see your struggle and feel it in the marrow of my bones.

I understand quite viscerally what being told that you're dumb, or simply incapable, feels like.

I, too, know pain, heartache.

But, like Langston Hughes before me,

I, too, sing love.

I too, sing joy.

As a Black Queer Teacher, my pedagogy is "all about love."

I dance love. I write love.

I poem love.

I share love.

I express love.

With all the evil and outright hatred leveled against queer people globally, we need a reminder of the spirit child in us, the spirit child that laughed and loved. Let us rehear Whitney Houston, "Greatest Love of All," one last time:

I believe the children are our future

Teach them well and let them lead the way

Show them all the beauty they possess inside

Give them a sense of pride to make it easier

Let the children's laughter remind us how we used to be

Love was always with me, especially at school—I just had to hear this love far above and against that hate that worked over time to drown out this love.

When I was in fourth grade, at Andrew A. Robinson Elementary School, the school located down the street from the Pic-N-Save that my mother ventured off to, I worked with the morning TV production team. This team, led by students at the school and mentored by the teachers and staff, helped to produce the morning and afternoon news broadcast. We chose, for that year, Des'ree's classic, "You Gotta Be." I LOVED that song, and still do. As I quote the lyrics at the start of this chapter:

> Listen as your day unfolds
> Challenge what the future holds
> Try and keep you head up to the sky
> Lovers, they may cause you tears
> Go ahead, release your fears
> Stand up and be counted
> Don't be ashamed to cry

Having "aged" a few years, I now understand the purpose and intent of "You Gotta Be," in ways that I didn't always understand Whitney Houston's "Greatest Love of All."

In "You Gotta Be," Des'ree encouraged us students, at Andrew Robinson, to be bold, to develop patience with ourselves, to "solve puzzles in our own time," and most importantly, to listen to our inner spirit—a spirt that center and drive our emotional well-being. The final message hits home:

> You gotta be bad, you gotta be bold, you
>   gotta be wiser
> You gotta be hard, you gotta be tough, you
>   gotta be stronger

You gotta be cool, you gotta be calm, you
    gotta stay together
All I know, all I know, love will save the day

As love's power followed me, its spirit shielded me against cruel forces. Yet, the composition of love and cruelty continues to teach me about the importance of living our days together, learning from each other, and investigating our past harms so that we heal and not repeat them. Love permits us to live with the beauty of our differences, in unity, together.

As Audre Lorde teaches us, "unity does not mean uniformity."

We are not a monolith, and never should we aspire to be. We each are unique and have within each of us powerful experiences that, when remembered and shared, can help radically inform, transform, and reshape society and our world. Our stories can, too, lead us back to love or toward it.

Forgiveness matters, too.

I love my mother to pieces, and loving her today brings me such peace.

I can look back on all the harm I endured as I came of age in the inner-city and continue to hate all those people. But what point would that serve? Who would that serve? Do I dislike them? Perhaps. Do I hate them. Not at all.

Our stories are lessons—gifts to change hearts.

Our stories are not easy. There is pain. There is hurt. There might even be lovelessness. But I encourage you, dear reader, to find the joy on the other end. Find joy through articulation. Through utterance.

Out of this pain craft power.

Craft possibility.

Craft love.

Figure 17 My best friend, Jennifer Petit-Homme, and I at my graduation from the University of Michigan. Ann Arbor, Michigan. We met as undergraduates at UF on the first day of our Haitian Creole class. She flew in from Florida. Jennifer, I love you so much. Thank you for being my best friend. You are love! Date: August 2015.

Instructional activities/ Discussion questions

- David writes about his younger life in the inner-city: growing up, stealing from the local store, attending the Boys & Girls Club and says he had fun. What are some misconceptions that society have about the neighborhood or neighborhoods that you grew up in? How can you write stories to combat those misconceptions?

- David has a long conversation with his mother about her leaving him and his siblings when he was young. Her actions hurt him and led to him experiencing various states of homelessness. If you had a chance to speak to someone who has harmed you—would you? What questions might you ask? Would you forgive them? Why or why not? How would you begin the process of forgiveness?

- David speaks a lot about the white teachers that he encountered and his perceptions of their racism and homophobia and belief in his academic abilities. Have you ever experienced a teacher who judged your academic potential based on your identity or identities—and particularly your race, gender, sexuality, language, or disability? If so, how did this judgment make you feel and how did you navigate this moment? Did you confront the moment—why or why not?

- David writes about some of his favorite writers, such as E. Lynn Harris, Audre Lorde, and James Baldwin. Were there any books or writers that helped you discover your identity/identities or helped you survive difficult times in your life? If so, and who are they? What are the names of these books? How did the writers help you discover your identity? How did they help you navigate difficult times?

- David uses three organizing themes to craft his story: the inner-city, mother, and school. If you had a chance to write your story, what three organizing themes would you select and why?

- David concludes that forgiveness and love are the key for living a happy and joyous life? Do you agree? Why or why not? What for you is love and forgiveness—how might you define these words and why?

Notes

1. Sonia Sanchez, *Shake Lose My Skin: New and Selected Poems*, p. 3; "Homecoming."

2. 69 Boyz, "Tootsie Roll." Watch Video here: https://www.yout ube.com/watch?v=qs7f3ssuEjA or listen here: https://www. youtube.com/watch?v=We0uI42CQGQ

3. "Browns Dump, Jacksonville, FL, Clean Up" https://cumulis. epa.gov/supercpad/SiteProfiles/index.cfm?fuseaction=sec ond.Cleanup&id=0401003#bkground

    Steve Patterson, "Long-Promised Jacksonville ash cleanup begins under scrutiny" https://www.jacksonville.com/story/ news/2010/01/27/long-promised-jacksonville-ash-cleanup-begins-under-scrutiny/15958180007/

4. Kristopher Brooks, "Sale of Bethune's Elementary Stalls Again" https://www.jacksonville.com/story/news/education/2012/ 10/08/sale-jacksonvilles-bethune-elementary-stalls-again/ 15851986007/

5. Environmental Protection Agency.

6. Federal Povery line: https://www.cdph.ca.gov/Programs/ CID/DOA/Pages/OA_ADAP_Federal_Poverty_Guideline_Ch art.aspx

7. Whitney Houston, "All At Once" from her debut album *Whitney Houston* (Arista Records, 1985).

8. Rooming Houses predates set ups such Air BnB and often operated like mini motels. The owner of these homes would rent rooms in their homes to people for any duration of time. There were no frills or glamour to the rooms. Often these were working class or poor Black people trying to make extra money in the very ways that people with Air BnB want to. The conditions of "Rooming Houses" were often subpar, but they

provided otherwise needed shelter for those who could not find and/or afford to rent their own apartment or homes.

9. My grandfather, Eddie, was, in fact, ill. On the days, nights, and weeks that I spent with him, I often changed his "bedpan," because he was too weak to make it across the hall to the bathroom; I laid out his pills each day—large pills, small pills. I changed and bandaged one of his big toes that he had surgery on; I emptied and cleaned his "spit bucket," received and prepared his "meals on wheels"; I made sure he did his daily breathing exercising—making sure that he inhaled enough so that the little blue ball reached the expected height. He played cards until his last days. He died shortly after I finished fourth grade. My mother briefly returned to Jacksonville to attend his funeral and left again. And for the first time in my life, I—though briefly—moved with my dad, who felt quite estranged at the time. I then quickly moved with my Aunt Kay Kay, to start fifth grade at Mary McLeod Bethune. I was devastated and spent many nights crying on the floor at my auntie's house. I was saddened by my grandfather's passing, he was in his early 70s. I was also enraged at my mother. I took this rage out on my fifth-grade teacher, the otherwise kind Mr Hill, before penning this anger in an essay competition, DARE.

10. WIC stands for Women, Infants and Children. See the following link for more information: https://www.fns.usda.gov/wic

11. Patrick Moynihan used policy to spread lies about Black mothers and the destruction of Black families. The policy influenced many that followed, including the war on drugs and DARE.

12. IB = International Baccalaureate Program. Stanton College Prep was, at the time, the only high school in Jacksonville with such a Program. The Paxon School of Advanced Studies would soon follow this path and create an IB Program that merely rivaled Stanton's. There are now four schools in Duval County that offers an IB Program. https://dcps.duvalschools.org/Page/5981.

13. Listen here to James Galway perform this beautiful piece. https://www.youtube.com/watch?v=iFjwsBoVsBo

14. Translated in English as "The Girl from Arles," de Georges Bizet's "2me Menuet De L' Arlésienne" serves as the Aria to playwright Alphonse Daudet's short story "L' Arlésienne," which he first published in 1869. In the short story, Daudet speaks of unrequited love, infidelity, and suicide. The girl Arles cheats on her lover, a "peasant" sailor named Fréderi. Unable to cope with discovering her infidelity, he "descents into madness" and completes suicide by jumping off his balcony. See more on L' Arlésienne at: https://en.wikipedia. org/wiki/L%27Arl%C3%A9sienne_(short_story)#:~:text= L'Arl%C3%A9sienne%2C%20which%20translates%20 to,by%20jumping%20off%20a%20balcony.

15. San Marco: https://en.wikipedia.org/wiki/San_Marco_(Jacks onville)

16. The National Blue Ribbon Schools Program recognizes public and private elementary, middle, and high schools based on their overall academic excellence or their progress in closing achievement gaps among student subgroups. The coveted National Blue Ribbon School award affirms the hard work of students, educators, families, and communities in creating safe and welcoming schools where students master challenging and engaging content. "National Blue Ribbon School," US Department of Education. See https://www2. ed.gov/programs/nclbbrs/index.html

17. Claude Steele, *Whistling Vivaldi: And How Other Cues about Stereotypes Affect Us.*

18. Patricia Williams, *The Alchemy of Race and Rights: Diary of a Law Professor.*

19. Taking a line from Essex Hemphill's poem, "Dream," my dissertation is titled, "Out of this Confusion I Bring My Heart: Love, Liberation, and the Rise and Black Lesbian and Gay Cultural Politics in Late Twentieth Century America" and you can

read it online here: https://deepblue.lib.umich.edu/handle/2027.42/113558?show=full

20. See Essex Hemphill's essay, "Loyalty" in *Ceremonies: Prose and Poetry*, to situate my reference to "ass-splitting truth." See Max Sherman, *Barbara Jordan: Speaking the Truth with Eloquent Thunder*.

21. Audre Lorde, "Litany for Survival" in *The Collected Poems of Audre Lorde*, p. 255.

22. Audre Lorde, "The Transformation of Silence into Language and Action," in *Sister Outsider*, p. 41.

23. Pat Parker, "Have You Ever Tried to Hide" in *Movement in Black*.

24. Cheryl Clarke, *The Days of Good Looks: Prose and Poetry, 1980-2005*.

25. Dignity. But I'd sang it like Whitney, stress the vernacular pronunciation of the word.

26. Ntozake Shange, "A Laying of Hands," in *For Colored Girls Who Have Considered Suicide When the Rainbow Is Enuf*.

27. The AIM Program served as a college access program for underrepresented minority students. The program admits students who demonstrate high academic achievement--via their Grade Point Average, or GPA, yet have SAT or ACT scores that fall below the national average. The AIM Program provided students an opportunity to acquaint themselves with college and required students to attend the Summer B semester, or second part of the Summer session. Students participated in summer enrichment programs and received additional support from mentors. Unfortunately, the AIM program no longer exists at UF. However, its sibling program PAACT does, thank god!

28. "UF student-scholar says McNair program is 'priceless.'" https://news.ufl.edu/archive/2007/02/uf-student-scholar-says-mcnair-program-is-priceless.html

Index

www.ingramcontent.com/pod-product-compliance
Lightning Source LLC
Chambersburg PA
CBHW070711280326
41926CB00089B/3928